Get Hooked on Crochet

Get Hooked on Crochet

FUN AND COLORFUL PATTERNS FOR BEGINNERS

Natalie Beard

CICO BOOKS

LONDON NEW YORK

To my beautiful girls, Rosie, Martha, Violet, and Audrey

Published in 2024 by CICO Books
an imprint of Ryland Peters & Small Ltd
341 E 116th St, New York, NY 10029

www.rylandpeters.com

10 9 8 7 6 5 4 3 2 1

Text © Natalie Beard 2024
Design, illustration, and photography
© CICO Books 2024

A CIP catalog record for this book is
available from the Library of Congress.

ISBN: 978 1 80065 369 6

Printed in China

Editor: Marie Clayton
Pattern checker: Carol Ibbetson
Designer: Alison Fenton
Photographer: James Gardiner
Equipment photographer: Martin Norris
Stylist: Nel Haynes
Illustrator: Stephen Dew

In-house editor: Jenny Dye
Art director: Sally Powell
Creative director: Leslie Harrington
Production manager: Gordana Simakov
Publishing manager: Carmel Edmonds

contents

Introduction 6
Tools and materials 8

introduction

I'm Natalie, a mom of four beautiful girls, and I am absolutely hooked on creating quirky crochet designs to entertain and make people smile.

I've loved to craft since I was little, and I have my mom to thank for that. I have early, happy memories of her pottery and her charcoal and pen-and-ink drawings filling our home. She still loves to knit for me and my daughters, and there's nothing quite like a cherished homemade gift.

Sadly, I lost my dad two months before having my third daughter, and I picked up a crochet hook as a means of coping with the mixed emotions from losing my dad and gaining a gorgeous new baby. I truly believe crochet is a happy distraction from day-to-day stresses, and is so good for our mental health and wellbeing, allowing you to escape to a squish-filled happy place!

I had my first commission from UK craft store Hobbycraft, and then had the pleasure of designing for Knitcraft (Hobbycraft's sister company). After being made redundant from my day job of 13 years, I decided to turn the negative into a positive and focus on crochet full-time! Ever since, I have been honored to work with lots of yarn companies, and have been on the design team for *Simply Crochet* magazine. I now also work as a Hobbycraft Artisan in store, where I host workshops.

My passion for crochet and all things yarny has grown into a total squishy obsession and I rarely go a day without getting my hook out. I hope you'll enjoy my yarn-filled adventure through the pages of my first-ever book, feel inspired to pick up your hook, and have heaps of fun making!

BEFORE YOU BEGIN

If you are new to crochet, check out the Techniques section on pages 114–125 and the Abbreviations on page 126. On page 8, you'll find a guide to the tools you'll need. Each of the projects has a skill rating, from Very Easy (one circle) to Easy (two circles), and Intermediate (three circles). Start with the Very Easy patterns, then move on to the next two levels once you know the basic techniques.

tools and materials

Here is a guide to the basic tools and materials you will need to make the projects in this book.

CROCHET HOOKS

A crochet hook is a simple tool that is shaped to fit in the hand and glide easily in and out of the crochet loops. Modern crochet hooks are made in bamboo, wood, aluminum, steel, casein, or plastic. Some have handles made of plastic and many have a flat piece around the center of the length of the hook, which is a thumb guide.

The choice of hook is up to you, but the varnish on bamboo crochet hooks can wear off after a while and they then catch on the yarn. You may find that an ergonomic hook with a round plastic handle (shown above) is more comfortable. Whichever type of hook you choose, it's important that it has a good smooth tip—for this reason alone it's worth buying one of the more expensive brands.

Crochet hooks come in a variety of sizes and you'll be guided by the pattern and the thickness of yarn as to which size you need.

OTHER TOOLS

As well your crochet hook, there are a few extra tools that you will need.

SHARP SCISSORS

Reserved for cutting yarn and thread only: do not cut paper with these, because it will quickly blunt them.

APE MEASURE

ou will need this to block some of
e finished projects to the finished
ze (see page 120).

PINS

Use rustproof, glass-headed, or
T-headed quilters' pins for blocking
and to pin crocheted pieces
together before you join them (see
pages 120–122). Bright-colored tops
will prevent the pins getting lost in
the crocheted fabric.

YARN

Yarns come in different thicknesses
or weights. The five basic types,
from lightest to heaviest, are
fingering (4-ply), light worsted
(double-knitting or DK), worsted
(Aran), bulky (chunky), and super
bulky (super chunky). The finer the
yarn, the smaller the hook size that
is needed—the pattern will suggest
a suitable hook size. Most ball
bands will also suggest a suitable
hook size for the yarn.

Yarns are available in a variety
of different fibers, from acrylic to
natural fibers such as 100% wool,
alpaca, cashmere, cotton, mohair,
and bamboo, as well as mixes of
different fibers. Acrylic is synthetic
and manufactured to imitate
wool yarn. Its advantages are that
it is cheaper than wool and other
natural fibers, and can be put in the
washing machine. Cotton is a soft
and strong yarn, and it makes a very
sturdy and consistent crocheted
fabric. Natural yarns such as wool,
cashmere, alpaca, and mohair are
softer and warmer. They are more
delicate and will often need to be
hand-washed.

If you wish, you can use different
yarns to the ones recommended in
this book, but you will need a yarn
with the same recommended hook
size as the pattern (see the Yarnsub
website on page 127 to help you).
Many of the patterns in this book
use only a small amount of each
color, so they're ideal for using up
yarn from your stash.

TITCH MARKERS

hese aren't essential but are
seful for clipping onto your
orking loop when you're taking
break partway through a project
that it doesn't unravel. They're
so handy for keeping track of how
any chains you've made when
arting a project and for marking
e start of a round.

YARN NEEDLE

This type of needle is longer and
thicker than a sewing needle. The
blunt end will not split the yarn
when sewing up and the large eye
makes it easier to thread with yarn.

CHAPTER 1
Colorful
Home Accessories

Brighten up your kitchen with this eye-catching and useful dish towel holder. Featuring floral granny squares, this design can be worked in any colorway and is perfect for using up leftover yarn from other projects.

dish towel tidy

YARN AND MATERIALS
Rico Ricorumi DK (100% cotton) light worsted (DK) weight yarn, 64yd (58m) per 1oz (25g) ball
1 ball in each of:
Yellow 006 (A)
Sky Blue 031 (B)
Red 028 (C)
Green 049 (D)
2 natural wooden rings, 2in (5cm) diameter

HOOK AND EQUIPMENT
US size C/2–D/3 (3mm) crochet hook
Yarn needle

FINISHED MEASUREMENT
7½in (19cm) long when folded incl rings x 3½in (9cm) wide

ABBREVIATIONS
See page 126.

HANGER
SQUARE
(make 2 in diff colors as specified)
Using A or B, make a magic ring.
Round 1: Ch3 (counts as 1dc), 11dc in magic ring. *(12 dc)*
Fasten off A, join C. Fasten off B, join A.
Round 2: Ch2 (does not count as a st), dc5tog in first st, ch2, [dc5tog in next st, ch2] 11 times, slst to first dc in beg dc5tog. *(12-dc cluster, 5 x ch-2)*
Fasten off C, join B. Fasten off A, join C.
Round 3: (Ch3 (counts as 1dc), 2dc, ch3, 3dc) in ch sp, [3hdc in next ch sp] twice, *(3dc, ch3, 3dc) in next ch sp, [3hdc in next ch sp] twice, rep from * twice more, slst in third ch of beg ch-3.
Fasten off all colors, join D to corner ch sp.
Round 4: (Ch3 (counts as first dc), 2dc, ch3, 3dc) in corner ch sp, [3dc in next ch sp] 3 times, *[3dc, ch3, 3dc] in corner ch sp, [3dc in next ch sp] 3 times, rep from * twice more, slst in third ch of beg ch.
Fasten off. Sew in ends (see page 120), sew two squares tog along one edge, using mattress stitch (see page 121).

ENDS
(make 2, working on opp short sides of rectangle)
With RS facing, join D to first st.
Row 1: Ch1, 1sc in each st to end, 1sc in ch sp, ch1, turn. *(16 sc)*
Row 2: 1sc in each st to end, ch1, turn.
Row 3: Sc2tog, 12sc, sc2tog, ch1, turn. *(14 sc)*
Row 4: 1sc in each st to end, ch1, turn.
Row 5: Sc2tog, 10sc, sc2tog, ch1, turn. *(12 sc)*
Row 6: 1sc in each st to end, ch1, turn.
Row 7: Sc2tog, 8sc, sc2tog, ch1, turn. *(10 sc)*
Row 8: 1sc in each st to end, ch1, turn.
Round 9: Sc2tog, 6sc, sc2tog, ch1, turn. *(8 sc)*
Round 10: 1sc in each st to end, ch1, turn.
Round 11: Sc2tog, 4sc, sc2tog, ch1, turn. *(6 sc)*
Round 12: 1sc in each st to end, ch1, turn.
Rounds 13–17: 1sc in each st to end, ch1, turn.
Round 18: 1sc in each st to end.
Fasten off, leaving long tail to sew around a wooden ring.
Rep on opp side.
Border: 1sc in each st and row end around all sides.
Fasten off.

FINISHING
Fold end over wooden ring and sew in place. Rep with second ring on other end of hanger.

flower pillow

Add a burst of color to any room with this unique pillow. The circular pattern features a repeated 3D-petal effect, making this pillow a statement piece for your home. Choose a selection of bulky yarns in bold contrasting shades.

SKILL RATING ● ● ○

YARN AND MATERIALS
Women's Institute Soft and Chunky (70% acrylic, 30% merino wool) bulky (chunky) weight yarn, 120yd (110m) per 3½oz (100g) ball

1 ball in each of:
Mustard (A)
Dusky Pink (B)
Pink (C)
2 balls of Petrol (D)

7½in (45cm) diameter circular pillow form

HOOK AND EQUIPMENT
US size L/11 (8mm) crochet hook
Yarn needle

FINISHED MEASUREMENTS
7½in (45cm) diameter
NOTE: First 3 rounds of front and back panels should measure approx. 6in (15cm)

ABBREVIATIONS
See page 126.

SPECIAL ABBREVIATION
Puff st (puff stitch): Yoh insert hook into specified st/sp, yoh and pull up a long loop, [yoh, insert hook in same st/sp, yoh and pull up a long loop] 3 times, yoh and pull through all 9 loops on hook, ch1 to close Puff st.

PILLOW
FLOWER
Using A, make a magic ring.
Round 1: Ch3 (counts as first dc), 11dc in magic ring, slst in third ch of beg ch. *(12 dc)*
Round 2: Working between dc from prev round, ch2 (does not count as st), [puff st, ch2] 12 times, slst in top of first puff st. *(12 puff sts, 12 x ch-2)*
Round 3: Ch2 (does not count as a st), [2hdc in ch-2 sp, 1hdc in puff st] 12 times, slst in first hdc. *(36 hdc)*
Fasten off A, join B.
Round 4: Ch1, [BPslst around hdc, ch3, miss next hdc] 18 times, slst to first slst.
Round 5: Working in each ch-3 sp from prev round, [slst into next ch-3 sp, ch3, 2dc, ch3, slst in same ch-3 sp] 18 times. Fasten off.
Round 6: Using B, join and work in missed hdcs from Round 4, ch 1, [BPslst around hdc, ch4, miss next hdc] 18 times, slst to first slst.
Round 7: Working in each ch-4 sp from prev round, [slst into next ch-4 sp, ch4, 3tr, ch4, slst in same 4-ch sp] 18 times. Fasten off B, join C around a slst from prev round.
Round 8: Working in BPslst from Round 7, [BPslst, ch3] 18 times, slst into first slst.
Round 9: Slst into next ch-3 sp, ch2 (does not count as a st), 3hdc in same ch-3 sp, [3hdc in next ch-3 sp] 17 times, slst into first hdc. *(54 hdc)*

Round 10: (Ch4, miss 2 hdc, slst in next hdc), 18 times, slst into first st.
Round 11: Working in each ch-4 sp from prev round, [slst into next ch-4 sp, ch3, 2dc, ch3, slst in same ch-4 sp] 18 times.
Round 12: Working in slst from Round 11 [BPslst, ch6, miss next slst] 9 times, slst in first BPslst.
Round 13: Working in ch-6 sp from prev round, [slst into next ch-6 sp, ch4, 5tr, ch4, slst in same ch-6 sp] 9 times.
Fasten off and sew in ends.

FRONT AND BACK PANELS
(make 2)
Using D, make a magic ring.
Round 1: Ch3 (counts as 1dc throughout), 11dc in magic ring, slst in third ch of beg ch. *(12 dc)*
Round 2: Ch3, 1dc in same st, [2dc in next st] 11 times, slst in third ch of beg ch. *(24 dc)*
Round 3: Ch3, 2dc in next st, [1dc, 2dc in next st] 11 times, slst in third ch of beg ch. *(36 dc)*
Round 4: Ch3, 1dc, 2dc in next st, [2dc, 2dc in next st] 11 times, slst in third ch of beg ch. *(48 dc)*
Round 5: Ch3, 2dc, 2dc in next st, [3dc, 2dc in next st] 11 times, slst in third ch of beg ch. *(60 dc)*
Round 6: Ch3, 3dc, 2dc in next st, [4dc, 2dc in next st] 11 times, slst in third ch of beg ch. *(72 dc)*
Round 7: Ch3, 4dc, 2dc in next st, [5dc, 2dc in next st] 11 times, slst in third ch of beg ch. *(84 dc)*
Round 8: Ch3, 5dc, 2dc in next st, [6dc, 2dc in next st] 11 times, slst in third ch of beg ch. *(96 dc)*
Round 9: Ch3, 95dc, slst in third ch of beg ch. *(96 dc)*
Fasten off and sew in ends (see page 12).

FINISHING
Work line of surface crochet (see page 123) using A in top of each st in Round 7 and B in top of each st in Round 8 of front panel. Sew flower motif on front panel.
With front and back panels WS tog, using D work sc through each st around, placing pillow form inside before completing seam (see page 122).
Work line of surface crochet using C in joining round.
Fasten off and sew in ends.

aturing cute strawberry and flower motifs, these mason
 covers would add a pop of color to your kitchen shelf.
ey also make wonderful gifts on top of jars of honey
 homemade jelly.

mason jar covers

SKILL RATING ● ● ○

YARN AND MATERIALS
Rico Ricorumi DK (100% cotton)
light worsted (DK) weight yarn,
64yd (58m) per 1oz (25g) ball
   1 ball in each of:
   Sky Blue 031 (A)
   Fuchsia 014 (B)
   Yellow 006 (C)
   Green 049 (D)
   Red 028 (E)
   White 001 (F)

HOOK AND EQUIPMENT
US size C/2–D/3 (3mm) crochet hook

Yarn needle

FINISHED MEASUREMENT
5½in (14cm) diameter

ABBREVIATIONS
See page 126.

COVER
(make 1 in A, 1 in B)
Make a magic ring.
Round 1: 6sc in magic ring. *(6 sc)*
Round 2: [2sc in next st] 6 times. *(12 sc)*
Round 3: [1sc, 2sc in next st] 6 times. *(18 sc)*
Round 4: [2sc, 2sc in next st] 6 times. *(24 sc)*
Round 5: [3sc, 2sc in next st] 6 times. *(30 sc)*
Round 6: [4sc, 2sc in next st] 6 times. *(36 sc)*
Round 7: [5sc, 2sc in next st] 6 times. *(42 sc)*
Round 8: [6sc, 2sc in next st]6 times. *(48 sc)*
Round 9: [7sc, 2sc in next st] 6 times. *(54 sc)*
Round 10: [8sc, 2sc in next st] 6 times. *(60 sc)*
Round 11: [9sc, 2sc in next st] 6 times. *(66 sc)*
Round 12: [1sc, ch2, miss 1 st] to end, slst in first sc.
Fasten off and sew in ends.

CORD
(make 1 in C, 1 in D)
Ch80.
Fasten off.

STRAWBERRY
Using E, make a magic ring.
Round 1: Ch3 (counts as 1dc), 12dc, slst in third ch of
beg ch. *(13 dc)*
Round 2: Miss first st, (1hdc, 1dc) in next dc, [3tr in next
dc] twice, [3dc in next dc] twice, (2dc, 1tr) in next dc,
ch1, (1tr, 2dc) in next dc, [3dc in next dc] twice, [3tr in
next dc] twice, (1dc, 1hdc) in next dc, slst in first st.
Fasten off leaving long tail to sew to cover.

STALK
Using D.
Round 1: [Ch4, 1sc in second ch from hook, 1sc in each
of next 2 ch] 3 times, slst in first st.
Fasten off leaving long tail to sew to strawberry.

FLOWER

Using C, make a magic ring.

Round 1: 6sc in magic ring. *(6 sc)*

Round 2: [2sc in next st] 6 times. *(12 sc)*

Round 3: [1sc, 2sc in next st] 6 times. *(18 sc)*

Fasten off C, join F.

Round 4: *(1sc, ch3, 2tr) in next sc, (2tr, ch3, 1sc) in next sc, 1sc in next sc; rep from * 5 more times, slst to first sc.

Fasten off leaving long tail to sew to cover.

FINISHING

Weave cord through Round 10 of each cover, leaving 3 sc between in and out points. Tie ends in bow.

With a small amount of F, stitch simple seeds onto strawberry before sewing onto first cover. Sew stalk to base of strawberry. Sew flower onto top of second cover.

tulips stationery pot

Transform a simple tin can into a pretty stationery pot for your desk.
As well as simple stripes crocheted in basic single crochet, this design
uses three-double-crochet clusters to create the raised tulip flower pattern.

SKILL RATING ● ● ○

YARN AND MATERIALS
Knitcraft Cotton Blend DK (50% cotton, 50% acrylic) light worsted (DK) weight yarn, 235yd (215m) per 3½oz (100g) ball
    1 ball in each of:
    Yellow 1008 (A)
    Teal 1002 (B)
    Hot Pink 1003 (C)

Tin can

HOOK AND EQUIPMENT
US size G/6 (4mm) crochet hook

Yarn needle

FINISHED MEASUREMENTS
4¼in (11cm) tall by 10in (25.5cm) circumference

ABBREVIATIONS
See page 126.

SPECIAL ABBREVIATION
3dcCL (three-double-crochet cluster): yoh, insert hook in st, yoh, pull through (3 loops on hook), yoh, pull through first 2 loops on hook (2 loops on hook), yoh, insert hook in same st, yoh, pull through (4 loops on hook), yoh, pull through first 2 loops on hook (3 loops on hook), yoh, insert hook in same st, yoh, pull through (5 loops on hook), yoh, pull through first 2 loops on hook (4 loops on hook), yoh, pull through all 4 loops on hook.

COVER
Worked from base up.
Using A, make a magic ring.
Round 1: 6sc in magic ring. *(6 sts)*
Round 2: [2sc in next st] 6 times. *(12 sts)*
Round 3: [1sc, 2sc in next st] 6 times. *(18 sts)*
Round 4: [2sc, 2sc in next st] 6 times. *(24 sts)*
Round 5: [3sc, 2sc in next st] 6 times. *(30 sts)*
Round 6: [4sc, 2sc in next st] 6 times. *(36 sts)*
Round 7: 1scBLO in each st around.
Rounds 8-10: 1sc in each st around.
Fasten off A, join B.
Round 11: Ch4 (counts as 1dc, ch1), 1dc in same st, miss 2 sc, *(1dc, ch1, 1dc) in next st, miss 2 sc; rep from * 10 more times, slst in third ch of beg 4-ch.
Fasten off B, join C in a ch sp.
Round 12: Ch2 (does not count as st), [3dcCL in ch sp, ch3] 12 times. *(12 tulips)*
Fasten off C, join A.
Round 13: 3sc in each ch sp around. *(36 sts)*
Round 14: 1sc in each st around.
Fasten off A, join B.
Rounds 15 and 16: 1sc in each st around.
Fasten off B, join A.
Rounds 17 and 18: 1sc in each st around.
Fasten off A, join B.
Round 19: Rep Round 11.
Fasten off B, join C.
Round 20: Rep Round 12.
Fasten off C, join A.
Round 21: Rep Round 13.
Rounds 22 and 23: 1sc in each st around.
Fasten off and sew in ends (see page 120).

FINISHING
Place cover over tin.

snail doorstop

This cute character would add a playful touch to your home or a child's bedroom. The different colors in the yarn give gorgeous details to the crocheted fabric, but you could use any bulky yarn. Why not try using different shades from your stash on the snail's spiral shell for a multicolored effect?

SKILL RATING ● ○ ○

YARN AND MATERIALS
Knitcraft Join the Dots Chunky (80% acrylic, 20% wool) bulky (chunky) weight yarn, 208yd (190m) per 3½oz (100g) ball
    1 ball in each of:
    Purple Print 1000 (A)
    Cream Print 1002 (B)
Fiber filling
Weighted filling for base of body
Pair of ½in (8mm) black safety eyes

HOOK AND EQUIPMENT
US size H/8 (5mm) crochet hook
Yarn needle

FINISHED MEASUREMENTS
11¾in (30cm) wide maximum, by 7in (18cm) tall

ABBREVIATIONS
See page 126.

SNAIL
SHELL
Using A, make a magic ring.
Round 1: 6sc in magic ring. *(6 sts)*
Round 2: [2sc in next st] 6 times. *(12 sts)*
Round 3: [1sc, 2sc in next st] 6 times. *(18 sts)*
Round 4: [2sc, 2sc in next st] 6 times. *(24 sts)*
Round 5: [3sc, 2sc in next st] 6 times. *(30 sts)*
Round 6: [4sc, 2sc in next st] 6 times. *(36 sts)*
Round 7: [5sc, 2sc in next st] 6 times. *(42 sts)*
Round 8: [6sc, 2sc in next st] 6 times. *(48 sts)*
Round 9: [7sc, 2sc in next st] 6 times. *(54 sts)*
Round 10: [8sc, 2sc in next st] 6 times. *(60 sts)*
Round 11: 1scBLO in each st around.
Rounds 12 and 13: 1sc in each st around.
Fasten off and sew in ends (see page 120).
Repeat Rounds 1–10 for other side of shell.
Fasten off leaving a long tail to sew to first part of shell.

BODY
Using B, make a magic ring.
Round 1: 6sc in magic ring. *(6 sts)*
Round 2: [2sc in next st] 6 times. *(12 sts)*
Round 3: [1sc, 2sc in next st] 6 times. *(18 sts)*
Start to stuff with fiber filling until Round 22, do not stuff between Rounds 22–42, then stuff between Rounds 43–48.
Rounds 4–44: 1sc in each st around.
Insert safety eyes between Rounds 6 and 7, 4 sts apart.
Round 45: [1sc, sc2tog] 6 times. *(12 sts)*
Rounds 46 and 47: 1sc in each st around.
Round 48: [Sc2tog] 6 times. *(6 sts)*
Fasten off and sew closed.

ANTENNAE

Using B, ch15.

Row 1: Slst in second ch from hook, 13slst.
(14 slst)

Sew in ends.

FINISHING

Sew both parts of shell together, stitching
back loops only. Fill with fiber filling and
weighted filling before sewing closed.
Sew in ends.
Thread antennae strip through top of head,
between Rounds 1 and 2, and sew in place.
Sew shell to body.

mushroom & acorn storage baskets

Perfect for storing anything from toys and stationery to yarn and craft supplies, these baskets would make fun additions to any room. Worked in bulky cotton yarn, they are quick and simple to make. The crab stitch detailing around each lid creates a twisted, rounded edge.

SKILL RATING ●●○

YARN AND MATERIALS
Knitcraft Return Of Mac Yarn (100% cotton) bulky (chunky) weight yarn, 88½yd (81m) per 7oz (200g) ball

For Mushroom Storage Basket:
    1 ball in Terracotta (A)
    2 balls in Ecru (B)
    Small amount of Khaki (C)

For Acorn Storage Basket:
    1 ball in Khaki (C)
    2 balls in Linen (D)
    Small amount of Terracotta (A)

2 pairs of 1in (22mm) black safety eyes

HOOK AND EQUIPMENT
US size 10mm (N/15) crochet hook

Yarn needle

FINISHED MEASUREMENTS
Mushroom basket: 6in (15cm) diameter x 9¾in (25cm) tall

Acorn basket: 6in (15cm) diameter x 7in (18cm) tall

ABBREVIATIONS
See page 126.

SPECIAL ABBREVIATION
Waistcoat st (waistcoat stitch): Work each sc in V between sts.
Crab st (crab stitch): Ch1, insert hook in st to right, yoh and pull through (2 loops on hook) yoh, pull through 2 loops.

MUSHROOM STORAGE BASKET
CAP
Work in waistcoat st throughout.
Using A, make a magic ring.
Round 1: 6sc in magic ring. *(6 sc)*
Round 2: [2sc in next st] 6 times. *(12 sc)*
Round 3: 1sc in each st around.
Round 4: [1sc, 2sc in next st] 6 times. *(18 sc)*
Round 5: 1sc in each st around.
Round 6: [2sc, 2sc in next st] 6 times. *(24 sc)*
Round 7: 1sc in each st around.
Round 8: [3sc, 2sc in next st] 6 times. *(30 sc)*
Round 9: 1sc in each st around.
Round 10: [4sc, 2sc in next st] 6 times. *(36 sc)*
Round 11: 1sc in each st around.
Round 12: [5sc, 2sc in next st] 6 times. *(42 sc)*
Round 13: 1sc in each st around.
Round 14: [6sc, 2sc in next st] 6 times. *(48 sc)*
Round 15: 1sc in each st around.
Round 16: [7sc, 2sc in next st] 6 times. *(60 sc)*
Round 17: 1sc in each st around.
Round 18: Crab st in each st to end. *(60 sts)*
Fasten off and sew in ends (see page 120).

BASE
Work in waistcoat st throughout.
Using B, make a magic ring.
Round 1: 6sc in magic ring. *(6 sc)*
Round 2: [2sc in next st] 6 times. *(12 sc)*
Round 3: [1sc, 2sc in next st] 6 times. *(18 sc)*
Round 4: [2sc, 2sc in next st] 6 times. *(24 sc)*
Round 5: [3sc, 2sc in next st] 6 times. *(30 sc)*
Round 6: [4sc, 2sc in next st] 6 times. *(36 sc)*
Round 7: [5sc, 2sc in next st] 6 times. *(42 sc)*

Round 8: 1scBLO in each st around.
Rounds 9–21: 1sc in each st around.
Round 22: Crab st in each st to end. *(42 sts)*
Fasten off and sew in ends.

SMALL SPOTS
(make 3)
Using B, make a magic ring.
Round 1: 6sc in magic ring. *(6 sc)*
Fasten off leaving long tail to sew to cap.

LARGE SPOTS
(make 2)
Using B, make a magic ring.
Round 1: 6sc in magic ring. *(6 sc)*
Round 2: [2sc in next st] 6 times. *(12 sc)*
Fasten off leaving long tail to sew to cap.

FINISHING
Insert safety eyes between Rounds 13 and 14 of base, 6 sts apart.
Using a small amount of C, sew a simple mouth between Rounds 13 and 14 of base, across 3 sts.
Sew spots onto cap.

ACORN STORAGE BASKET
ACORN CAP
Work in waistcoat st throughout.
Using C, make a magic ring.
Round 1: 6sc in magic ring. *(6 sc)*
Round 2: [2sc in next st] 6 times. *(12 sc)*
Round 3: [1sc, 2sc in next st] 6 times. *(18 sc)*
Round 4: [2sc, 2sc in next st] 6 times. *(24 sc)*
Round 5: [3sc, 2sc in next st] 6 times. *(30 sc)*
Round 6: [4sc, 2sc in next st] 6 times. *(36 sc)*
Round 7: [5sc, 2sc in next st] 6 times. *(42 sc)*
Round 8: [6sc, 2sc in next st] 6 times. *(48 sc)*
Rounds 9–15: 1sc in each st around.
Round 16: Crab st in each st to end. *(48 sts)*
Fasten off and sew in ends.

ACORN STALK
Using C, ch4.
Row 1: Slst in second ch from hook, 2slst. *(3 sts)*
Fasten off leaving a long tail to sew to cap.

ACORN
Work in waistcoat st throughout.
Using D, make a magic ring.
Round 1: 6sc in magic ring. *(6 sc)*
Round 2: [2sc in next st] 6 times. *(12 sc)*
Round 3: 1sc in each st around.
Round 4: [1sc, 2sc in next st] 6 times. *(18 sc)*
Round 5: [2sc, 2sc in next st] 6 times. *(24 sc)*
Round 6: [3sc, 2sc in next st] 6 times. *(30 sc)*
Round 7: [4sc, 2sc in next st] 6 times. *(36 sc)*
Round 8: [5sc, 2sc in next st] 6 times. *(42 sc)*
Rounds 9–25: 1sc in each st around.
Round 26: Crab st in each st to end. *(42 sts)*
Fasten off and sew in ends.

FINISHING
Insert safety eyes between Rounds 12 and 13 of acorn, 6 sts apart.
Using a small amount of A, sew a simple mouth between Rounds 12 and 13 of acorn, across 3 sts.
Sew acorn stalk to top of acorn cap.

Add a gorgeous handmade detail to a bedroom or nursery with this multicolored rug. Crocheted with three strands of light worsted yarn held together, the pattern works up quickly and is finished with a pretty white edging. Choose bright shades like this version, or experiment with color by using pastel rainbow yarns.

rainbow rug

ILL RATING ● ● ○ ○

RN AND MATERIALS
men's Institute Premium Acrylic Yarn
0% acrylic) light worsted (DK) weight
rn, 273yd (250m) per 3½oz (100g) ball
ball in each of:
Bright Lilac 1007 (A)
Soft Blue 1025 (B)
Green 1001 (C)
Yellow 1025 (D)
Orange 1002 (E)
Red 1015 (F)
Soft Pink 1026 (G)
White 1000 (H)

OK AND EQUIPMENT
size L/11 (8mm) crochet hook
rn needle

NISHED MEASUREMENTS
aight edge: 33½in (85cm)
dius: 18in (46cm)

BREVIATIONS
e page 126.

RUG

Use three strands of each color held together.
Using A, ch7.
Row 1 (RS): 1sc in second ch from hook, 4sc, 3sc in last ch, working along opp side of chain, 5sc, turn. (*13 sc*)
Row 2: Ch1 (does not count as st throughout), 5sc, [2sc in next st] 3 times, 5sc, turn. (*16 sc*)
Row 3: Ch1, 5sc, [1sc, 2sc in next st] 3 times, 5sc, turn. (*19 sc*)
Row 4: Ch1, 5sc, [2sc, 2sc in next st] 3 times, 5sc, turn. (*22 sc*)
Row 5: Ch1, 5sc, [3sc, 2sc in next st] 3 times, 5sc, turn. (*25 sc*)
Fasten off A, join B.
Row 6: Ch1, 5sc, [4sc, 2sc in next st] 3 times, 5sc, turn. (*28 sc*)
Row 7: Ch1, 5sc, [5sc, 2sc in next st] 3 times, 5sc, turn. (*31 sc*)
Row 8: Ch1, 8sc, 2sc in next st, [6sc, 2sc in next st] twice, 8sc, turn. (*34 sc*)
Row 9: Ch1, 5sc, [7sc, 2sc in next st] 3 times, 5sc, turn. (*37 sc*)
Row 10: Ch1, 9sc, 2sc in next st, [8sc, 2sc in next st] twice, 9sc, turn. (*40 sc*)
Fasten off B, join C.
Row 11: Ch1, 5sc, [9sc, 2sc in next st] 3 times, 5sc, turn. (*43 sc*)
Row 12: Ch1, [10sc, 2sc in next st] 3 times, 10sc, turn. (*46 sc*)
Row 13: Ch1, 5sc, [11sc, 2sc in next st] 3 times, 5sc, turn. (*49 sc*)
Row 14: Ch1, 11sc, 2sc in next st, [12sc, 2sc in next st] twice, 11sc, turn. (*52 sc*)
Row 15: Ch1, 5sc, [13sc, 2sc in next st] 3 times, 5sc, turn. (*55 sc*)
Fasten off C, join D.
Row 16: Ch1, 13sc, 2sc in next st, [14sc, 2sc in next st] twice, 11sc, turn. (*58 sc*)
Row 17: Ch1, 5sc, [15sc, 2sc in next st] 3 times, 5sc, turn. (*61 sc*)

Row 18: Ch1, 13sc, 2sc in next st, [16sc, 2sc in next st] twice, 13sc, turn. (*64 sc*)
Row 19: Ch1, 5sc, [17sc, 2sc in next st] 3 times, 5sc, turn. (*67 sc*)
Row 20: Ch1, 14sc, 2sc in next st, [18sc, 2sc in next st] twice, 14sc, turn. (*70 sc*)
Fasten off D, join E.
Row 21: Ch1, 5sc, [19sc, 2sc in next st] 3 times, 5sc, turn. (*73 sc*)
Row 22: Ch1, 15sc, 2sc in next st, [20sc, 2sc in next st] twice, 15sc, turn. (*76 sc*)
Row 23: Ch1, 5sc, [21sc, 2sc in next st] 3 times, 5sc, turn. (*79 sc*)
Row 24: Ch1, 16sc, 2sc in next st, [22sc, 2sc in next st] twice, 10sc, 2sc in next st, 5sc, turn. (*83 sc*)
Row 25: Ch1, 5sc, [23sc, 2sc in next st] 3 times, 6sc, turn. (*86 sc*)
Fasten off E, join F.
Row 26: Ch1, 17sc, 2sc in next st, [24sc, 2sc in next st] twice, 12sc, 2sc in next st, 5sc, turn. (*90 sc*)
Row 27: Ch1, 5sc, [25sc, 2sc in next st] 3 times, 7sc, turn. (*93 sc*)
Row 28: Ch1, 18sc, 2sc in next st, [26sc, 2sc in next st] twice, 13sc, 2sc in next st, 6sc, turn. (*97 sc*)
Row 29: Ch1, 5sc, [27sc, 2sc in next st] twice, 30sc, 2sc in next st, 5sc, turn. (*100 sc*)
Row 30: Ch1, 19sc, 2sc in next st, [28sc, 2sc in next st] twice, 14sc, 2sc in next st, 7sc, turn. (*104 sc*)
Fasten off F, join G.

Row 31: Ch1, 74sc, 2sc in next st, 23sc, 2sc in next st, 5sc, turn. (*106 sc*)
Row 32: Ch1, 20sc, 2sc in next st, [30sc, 2sc in next st] twice, 17sc, 2sc in next st, 5sc, turn. (*110 sc*)
Row 33: Ch1, 41sc, 2sc in next st, 36sc, 2sc in next st, 25sc, 2sc in next st, 5sc, turn. (*113 sc*)
Row 34: Ch1, 21sc, 2sc in next st, [32sc, 2sc in next st] twice, 19sc, 2sc in next st, 5sc, turn. (*117 sc*)
Row 35: Ch1, 38sc, 2sc in next st, 37sc, 2sc in next st, 34sc, 2sc in next st, 5sc, turn. (*120 sc*)
Fasten off G.
With RS facing, join H to the bottom right corner.
Round 36: Ch1, (1sc, ch3, 1sc) in first corner, [ch3, miss 1 st, 1sc] 59 times, (1sc, ch3, 1sc) in next corner, [ch3, miss 1 row end, 1sc in next row end] 34 times, ch3, miss 1 row end, sl st in first st to join.
Fasten off.

FINISHING
Sew in all ends (see page 120).

granny stitch placemats and coasters

Try out the classic granny stitch with this simple and bold pattern. Mix and match your colors for each mat, or create coordinating ones with just two shades. A set of these placemats and coasters would make a lovely housewarming gift.

SKILL RATING ● ○ ○

YARN AND MATERIALS
Stitchcraft Cotton Blend DK
(50% cotton, 50% acrylic) light
worsted (DK) weight yarn, 235yd
(215m) per 3½oz (100g) ball
1 ball in each of:
Hot Pink (1003)
Red (1001)
Coral (1007)
Bright Blue (1005)
Mustard (1001)
Yellow (1008)
Teal (1002)
Lilac (1006)

HOOK AND EQUIPMENT
US size G/6 (4mm) crochet hook
Yarn needle

FINISHED MEASUREMENTS
Approx 12½in (31cm) diameter

ABBREVIATIONS
See page 126.

PLACEMAT

Using main color, make a magic ring.
Round 1: Ch3 (counts as first dc throughout), 2dc in ring, ch1, [3dc in ring, ch1] 5 times, slst in third ch of beg ch to join. (*six 3dc groups*)
Work in ch sp between dc groups from prev rounds throughout.
Round 2: Ch3 in first ch sp, [(3dc, ch1, 3dc) in next ch sp, ch1] 5 times, (3dc, ch1, 2dc) in first ch sp, slst in third ch of beg ch to join, slst in next ch sp. (*twelve 3dc groups*)
Round 3: (Ch3, 2dc) in same ch sp, ch1, [3dc in next ch sp, ch1] 11 times, slst in third ch of beg ch to join. (*twelve 3dc groups*)
Round 4: Ch3 in first ch sp, [3dc in next ch sp, ch2] 11 times, 3dc in first ch sp, slst in third ch of beg ch to join, slst in next ch sp. (*twelve 3dc groups*)
Round 5: (Ch3, 2dc, ch1, 3dc) in same ch sp, ch2, 3dc in next ch sp, ch2, [(3dc, ch1, 3dc) in next ch sp, ch2, 3dc in next ch sp, ch2] 5 times, slst in third ch of beg ch to join. (*eighteen 3dc groups*)
Round 6: Ch3 in first ch sp, [3dc in next ch sp, ch2] 17 times, 2dc in first ch sp, slst in third ch of beg ch to join, slst in next ch sp. (*eighteen 3dc groups*)
Round 7: (Ch3, 3dc) in same ch sp, ch2, [4dc in next ch sp, ch2] 17 times, slst in third ch of beg ch to join. (*eighteen 4dc groups*)
Round 8: Ch3 in first ch sp, [4dc in next ch sp, ch2] 17 times, 3dc in first ch sp, slst in third ch of beg ch to join, slst in next ch sp. (*eighteen 4dc groups*)
Round 9: (Ch3, 1dc, ch1, 2dc) in same ch sp, ch2, [(2dc, ch1, 2dc) in next ch sp, ch2] 17 times, slst in third ch of beg ch to join. (*thirty-six 2dc groups*)
Round 10: Ch3 in first ch sp, ch2, [3dc in next ch-sp, ch2] 35 times, 2dc in first ch sp, slst in third ch of beg ch. (*thirty-six 3dc groups*)
Fasten off main color, join contrasting color in any ch sp.

BORDER

Round 11: Ch1, 1sc in same ch sp, ch4, [1sc in next ch-sp, ch4] 35 times, slst in first ch to join, slst into next ch sp. (*36 sc, thirty-six 4-ch sp*)
Round 12: (1sc, 1hdc, 1dc, 1hdc, 1sc) in each 4-ch sp around, slst in top of sc from prev round. (*36 petals*)
Fasten off.

COASTER

Using main color, make a magic ring.
Round 1: Ch3 (counts as first dc throughout), 2dc in ring, ch1, [3dc in ring, ch1] 5 times, slst in third ch of beg ch to join. (*six 3dc groups*)
Work in ch sp between dc groups from prev rounds throughout.
Round 2: Ch3 in first ch sp, [(3dc, ch1, 3dc) in next ch sp, ch1] 5 times, (3dc, ch1, 2dc) in first ch sp, slst in third ch of beg ch to join, slst in next ch sp. (*twelve 3dc groups*)
Round 3: (Ch3, 2dc) in same ch sp, ch1, [3dc in next ch sp, ch1] 11 times, slst in third ch of beg ch to join. (*twelve 3dc groups*)

BORDER

Round 4: Ch1, 1sc in same ch sp, ch4, [1sc in next ch-sp, ch4] 11 times, slst in first ch to join, slst into next ch sp. (*12 sc, twelve 4-ch sp*)
Round 5: (1sc, 1hdc, 1dc, 1hdc, 1sc) in each 4-ch sp around, slst in top of sc from prev round. (*12 petals*)
Fasten off.

FINISHING

Sew in ends (see page 120).

Make this sweet caterpillar to keep your home warm and add a burst of color to your décor. The pattern uses simple single crochet stitches to create the 3D shape, and is finished with cute face details and antennae.

caterpillar draft excluder

SKILL RATING ● ● ●

YARN AND MATERIALS
Women's Institute Premium Acrylic Yarn (100% acrylic) light worsted (DK) weight yarn, 273yd (250cm) per 3½oz (100g) ball
   1 ball in each of:
   Red 1015 (A)
   Orange 1002 (B)
   Yellow 1025 (C)
   Green 1001 (D)
   Soft Blue 1025 (E)
   Magenta 1031 (F)
   Soft Pink 1026 (G)
Small amount of black light worsted (DK) yarn
Pair of safety eyes
Fiber filling

HOOK AND EQUIPMENT
US size L/11 (8mm) crochet hook
Yarn needle

FINISHED MEASUREMENTS
24¾in (63cm) long by 11in (28cm) circumference

ABBREVIATIONS
See page 126.

CATERPILLAR
Use three strands of each color held together.
Using A, make a magic ring.
Round 1: 6sc in ring. *(6 sc)*
Round 2: 2sc in each st. *(12 sc)*
Round 3: [1sc, 2sc in next st] 6 times. *(18 sc)*
Round 4: [2sc, 2sc in next st] 6 times. *(24 sc)*
Round 5: [3sc, 2sc in next st] 6 times. *(30 sc)*
Insert safety eyes between Rounds 3 and 4, 10 sts apart.
Rounds 6–9: 1sc in each st.
Round 10: [3sc, sc2tog] 6 times. *(24 sc)*
Round 11: [2sc, sc2tog] 6 times. *(18 sc)*
Round 12: [1sc, sc2tog] 6 times. *(12 sc)*
Start to stuff with fiber filling.
Fasten off A, join B.
Rounds 13–22: Rep Rounds 3–12.
Cont to stuff with fiber filling.
Fasten off B, join C.
Rounds 23–32: Rep Rounds 3–12.
Cont to stuff with fiber filling.
Fasten off C, join D.
Rounds 33–42: Rep Rounds 3–12.
Cont to stuff with fiber filling.
Fasten off D, join E.
Rounds 43–52: Rep Rounds 3–12.
Cont to stuff with fiber filling.

...sten off E, join F.
...unds 53–62: Rep Rounds 3–12.
...nt to stuff with fiber filling.
...sten off F, join G.
...unds 63–72: Rep Rounds 3–12.
...und 73: [Sc2tog] 6 times. *(6 sc)*
...ish stuffing, fasten off and sew
...p closed.

...TENNAE

...e a single strand of black yarn.
...35.
...w 1: Slst in second ch from hook,
...slst. *(34 slst)*

FINISHING

Sew in all ends (see page 12).
Thread antennae strip through top
of head, between Rounds 5 and 6,
and sew in place.
Using a single strand of black yarn,
sew mouth onto front of head.

caterpillar draft excluder **33**

Keep your books, magazines, and TV remote close to hand with this pretty and practical design. If you've mastered the basics of crochet and want to expand your skills, this pattern is a great way of trying out granny squares, 3D bobble stitches, and tassels.

granny square couch tidy

SKILL RATING ● ● ●

YARN AND MATERIALS
Women's Institute Premium Acrylic Yarn (100% acrylic) light worsted (DK) weight yarn, 273yd (250m) per 3½oz (100g) ball
    1 ball in each of:
    Soft Blue 1025
    Orange 1002
    Green 1001
    Red 1015
    Yellow 1005 (A)
    Blue 1024 (B)
    Cream 1004 (C)
    Soft Pink 1026 (D)
8in (20cm) wide piece of card

HOOK AND EQUIPMENT
US size G/6 (4mm) crochet hook
Yarn needle

FINISHED MEASUREMENTS
20in (51cm) long x 14in (36cm) wide

ABBREVIATIONS
See page 126.

SPECIAL ABBREVIATION
2dcCL (two-double-crochet cluster): yoh, insert hook in st, yoh, pull through (3 loops on hook), yoh, pull through first 2 loops on hook (2 loops on hook), yoh, insert hook in same st, yoh, pull through (4 loops on hook), yoh, pull through first 2 loops on hook (3 loops on hook), yoh, pull through all 3 loops on hook.

3dcCL (three-double-crochet cluster): yoh, insert hook in st, yoh, pull through (3 loops on hook), yoh, pull through first 2 loops on hook (2 loops on hook), yoh, insert hook in same st, yoh, pull through (4 loops on hook), yoh, pull through first 2 loops on hook (3 loops on hook), yoh, insert hook in same st, yoh, pull through (5 loops on hook), yoh, pull through first 2 loops on hook (4 loops on hook), yoh, pull through all 4 loops on hook.

Bobble: yoh, insert hook in st, yoh, pull through (3 loops on hook), yoh, pull through first 2 loops on hook (2 loops on hook), yoh, insert hook in same st, yoh, pull through (4 loops on hook), yoh, pull through first 2 loops on hook (3 loops on hook), yoh, insert hook in same st, yoh, pull through (5 loops on hook), yoh, pull through first 2 loops on hook (4 loops on hook), yoh, insert hook in same st, yoh, pull through (6 loops on hook), yoh, pull through first 2 loops on hook (5 loops on hook), yoh, insert hook in same st, yoh, pull through (7 loops on hook), yoh, pull through first 2 loops on hook (6 loops on hook), yoh, pull through all 6 loops on hook.

COUCH TIDY

SQUARES

(make 4 in assorted colors other than A, B, C, or D)
Using first color, make a magic ring.
Round 1: Ch3, 1dc in ring, (counts as one 2dcCL), ch1, [2dcCL, ch1] 7 times in ring, slst in first st. *(8 2dcCL, 8 ch sps)*
Fasten off first color, join second color in any ch sp.
Round 2: Working in ch sps from prev round, ch3, 2dc in first ch sp (counts as one 3dcCL), ch1, [3dcCL, ch1] 7 times, slst in first st. *(8 3dcCL, 8 ch sps)*
Fasten off second color, join third color in any ch sp.
Round 3: Working in ch sps from prev round, ch3 (counts as 1 dc), (2dc, ch2, 3dc) in first ch sp (corner), 3dc in next ch sp, *(3dc, ch2, 3dc) in next ch sp (corner), 3dc in next ch sp; rep from * twice, slst in first st. *(12 x 3dc groups, 4ch sps)*
Place 4 squares in a line and sew together using mattress stitch (see page 121).

Top border

Join A in top RH corner of row of squares.
Row 1 (RS): Ch1 (does not count as a st throughout), 1sc in each st, ch sp and gap between 3dc groups along edge of squares to LH corner of last square, turn. *(52 sc)*

Rows 2 and 3: Ch1, 1hdc in each st, turn.
Join B, do not fasten off A.
Carry yarn not in use within each st as you make it.
Row 4 (WS): Ch1, [3sc in A, Bobble in B] 12 times, 4sc in A, turn.
Fasten off B, do not fasten off A.
Rows 5 and 6: Ch1, 1hdc in each st, turn.
Row 7: Ch1, 1sc in each st.
Fasten off A.

Main section

Rotate to work along opp side of squares. Join C in RH corner of first square.
Row 1 (RS): Ch1 (does not count as a st throughout), 1sc in each st, ch sp and gap between 3dc groups along edge of squares to LH corner of last square, turn. *(52 sc)*
Rows 2–61: Ch1, 52hdc.
Fasten off C, join A.

Bottom border

Row 1 (WS): Ch1, 1sc in each st, turn. *(52 sc)*
Rows 2 and 3: Ch1, 1hdc in each st, turn.
Join B, do not fasten off A.
Carry yarn not in use within each st as you make it.
Row 4 (RS, will get folded to WS): Ch1, [3sc in A, Bobble in B] 12 times, 4sc in A, turn.
Fasten off B, do not fasten off A.
Rows 5 and 6: Ch1, 1hdc in each st, turn.
Fasten off A and sew in ends.

FINISHING

Fold top border of couch tidy approximately a quarter up main section.
Join C in top corner.
Row 1: Ch1, 1sc in each row end of main body to folded section, 1sc in each row end through both layers to create the pocket.
Fasten off and sew in ends.
Rep on other side.

TASSELS

(make 2)
Wrap D around card approximately 20 times.
Tie all strands at tip with length of D yarn, leaving tail to sew to corners of couch tidy.
Gently pull all strands from card and cut loops at opp end.
A third down from top, wrap a length of A four to six times around and knot securely.
Sew a tassel to each pocket bottom corner.

Made in beautiful vibrant colors, this wall tidy is ideal for storing anything from books and gift wrap to clothes and toys. The flower petals add a unique detail to the traditional granny squares.

flower square wall tidy

YARN AND MATERIALS

Knitcraft Cotton Blend DK (50% cotton, 50% acrylic) light worsted (DK) weight yarn, 235yd (215m) per 3½oz (100g) ball
 1 ball in each of:
 Hot Pink 1003 (A)
 Yellow 1008 (B)
 Bright Blue 1005 (C)
 Red 1001 (D)
 Teal 1002 (E)

2 lengths of dowel, each 12in (30.5cm) long

HOOK AND EQUIPMENT

US size G/6 (4mm) crochet hook

Yarn needle

FINISHED MEASUREMENTS

29cm (11½in) wide by 30cm (11¾in) tall when folded

ABBREVIATIONS

See page 126.

SPECIAL ABBREVIATION

Standing sc: Wrap new yarn over hook from the back twice. Insert hook into stitch, yoh and pull up a loop. Complete sc as normal.

WALL TIDY

SQUARES

(make 3)

Using A, make a magic ring.

Round 1: Ch4 (counts as 1dc, ch1), [1dc in ring, ch1] 11 times, slst in third ch of beg 4-ch to join. *(12 dc, twelve 1-ch sp)*

Fasten off A, join B with a standing sc in any ch sp.

Round 2: Ch2, [1sc in next 1-ch sp, ch2] 11 times, slst in first sc to join. *(12 sc, twelve 2-ch sp)*

Fasten off B, join C with a standing sc around BP of any sc from Round 2.

Round 3: Ch2, [1sc around BP of next sc, ch2] 11 times, slst in first sc to join. *(12 sc, twelve 2-ch sp)*

Round 4: Slst in next 2-ch sp, ch3 (counts as 1dc), (2dc, ch2, 3dc) in same sp, [2dc in next 2-ch sp] twice, *(3dc, ch2, 3dc) in next 2-ch sp, [2dc in next 2-ch sp] twice; rep from * twice, slst in first dc to join.

Fasten off C, join B in any corner sp from Round 4.

Round 5: (Ch 3, 2dc, ch2, 3dc) in corner ch sp, [3dc between next two dc groups] 3 times, *(3dc, ch2, 3dc) in corner ch sp, [3dc between next two dc groups] 3 times; rep from * twice, slst in first dc to join.

Fasten off B, join D in any 2-ch sp of Round 2.

Round 6: *(Slst, ch2, 2dc, ch2, slst) in 2-ch sp; rep from * 11 times, slst in first slst to join. *(12 petals)*

Fasten off D.

Place 3 squares in a line and sew together using mattress stitch (see page 121).

First channel

Working in tops of squares, join A in top RH corner ch sp.

Row 1: Ch3 (counts as 1dc), 1dc in same sp, 3dc in each sp between 3dc groups on top edge of squares and 3dc in each join between squares, 2dc in corner ch sp, ch2, turn. *(Fourteen 3dc groups, two 2dc groups)*

Rows 2–5: 1hdc in each st to the end, ch2, turn. *(46 hdc)* Fasten off leaving a long tail.

Granny stripe section

Join A to opp side of squares in top RH corner ch sp.

Row 1: Ch3, 1dc in same sp, 3dc between each pair of dc groups, 2dc in last ch sp. *(Fourteen 3dc groups, two 2dc groups)*

Fasten off A. Join C.

Row 2: Ch3, 3dc between each pair of dc groups, 1dc in last dc. *(Fifteen 3dc groups, 2dc)*

Fasten off C. Join B.

Row 3: Repeat Row 1.

Fasten off B. Join D.

Row 4: Repeat Row 2.

Fasten off D, join E with RS facing.

Main section

Rows 5–44: Ch2 (counts as first hdc), 1hdc in each st to end, ch2, turn. *(47 hdc)*

Row 45: Ch2 (counts as first hdc), 1hdc in each st to end.

Fasten off leaving a long tail.

Fold first channel section in A over to WS and sew edge to Row 1 to form a channel for one dowel. Fold four rows of main section over to WS and sew to create channel for second dowel.

Border

Join E to any row edge.

Round 1: Work sc along side edge evenly spaced across the row ends. Repeat for second edge.

Fasten off and sew in ends (see page 120).

HANGING CHAINS

Using E, make two lengths of 30ch and one length of 50ch.

Starting in the second st from hook, work 1slst in each ch. Fasten off leaving a long tail for each length to sew onto tidy.

FINISHING

Lay tidy flat with RS of squares facing down. Fold squares and striped section up over main section. Sew one end of a 30-ch length to end of first channel at one end and other end to end of second channel at matching end (see photograph for guidance). Repeat with second 30-ch length on other side. Sew ends of 50-ch length to opposite sides at top of second channel.

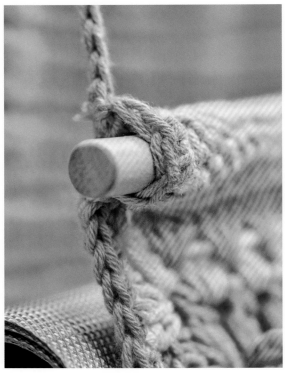

under the rainbow blanket

Get cozy with this showstopping blanket design. Each of the squares could be worked up when you have a spare evening. The pieces are then sewn together and a rainbow border is added for the finishing touch.

ARN AND MATERIALS

omen's Institute Premium Acrylic
arn (100% acrylic) light worsted (DK)
eight yarn, 273yd (250m) per 3½oz
00g) ball

1 ball in each of:
Yellow 1005 (A)
Soft Blue 1025 (C)
Green 1001 (D)
Orange 1002 (E)
Red 1024 (F)

2 balls in each of:
Soft Pink 1026 (B)
Petrol 1029 (G)

HOOK AND EQUIPMENT

US size G/6 (4mm) crochet hook
Yarn needle

FINISHED MEASUREMENTS

41½in (104cm) square

ABBREVIATIONS

See page 126.

SPECIAL ABBREVIATION

Picot: Ch3, slst in second ch from hook, slst in next ch.

UNSHINE SQUARE

(make 4)

sing A, make a magic ring.

Round 1: Ch3 (counts as 1dc throughout), 11dc in ring, st in top of beg 3-ch to join. *(12 dc)*

Round 2: Ch3, 1dc in same st, [2dc in next st] 11 times, lst in top of beg 3-ch to join. *(24 dc)*

Round 3: Ch3, 2dc in next st, [1dc, 2dc in next st] times, slst in top of beg 3-ch to join. *(36 dc)*

Round 4: *SlstFLO, (1dcFLO, picot, 1dcFLO) in next st, stFLO; rep from * 11 times, slst in beg slst to join. asten off A, join B in any unworked back loop om Round 4.

Round 5: Ch3, 1dcBLO, 4hdcBLO, 2dcBLO, (2dcBLO, ch2, dcBLO) in next st (corner), *2dcBLO, 4hdcBLO, 2dcBLO, dcBLO, ch2, 2dcBLO) in next st; rep from * twice ore, slst in top ch of beg 3-ch to join. *(32 dc, 16 hdc, ur 2-ch sp)*

Round 6: Ch3, 1dc in each st and (2dc, ch2, 2dc) in ch corner sp, slst in top of beg 3-ch to join. 4 dc, four 2-ch sp)

Round 7: Rep Round 6. (80 dc, four 2-ch sp) asten off B, join C in corner sp.

Round 8: (Ch3, 2dc, ch2, 3dc) in same corner sp, [miss ext 2 sts, 3dc in next st] 6 times, ** miss next 2 sts, dc, ch2, 3dc) in corner sp, [miss next 2 sts, 3dc in next] 6 times; rep from ** twice more, miss last 2 sts, st in top of beg 3-ch to join. *(96 dc, four 2-ch sp)* asten off and sew in ends (see page 120).

RAINBOW SQUARE

(make 4)

Using B, make a magic ring.

Row 1: Ch3 (counts as 1dc throughout), 2dc in ring. (3 dc)
Fasten off B, join C.

Row 2: Ch3, turn, 1dc in same st, [2dc in next st] twice. *(6 dc)*
Fasten off C, join D.

Row 3: Ch3, turn, 2dc in next st, [1dc, 2dc in next st] twice. *(9 dc)*
Fasten off D, join A.

Row 4: Ch3, turn, 1dc, 2dc in next st, [2dc, 2dc in next st] twice. *(12 dc)*
Fasten off A, join E.

Row 5: Ch3, turn, 2dc, 2dc in next st, [3dc, 2dc in next st] twice. *(15 dc)*
Fasten off E, join F.

Row 6: Ch3, turn, 3dc, 2dc in next st, [4dc, 2dc in next st] twice. *(18 dc)*
Fasten off F, join B.

Row 7: Ch3, turn, 4dc, 2dc in next st, [5dc, 2dc in next st] twice. *(21 dc)*
Fasten off B, join C.

Row 8: Ch3, turn, 5dc, 2dc in next st, [6dc, 2dc in next st] twice. *(24 dc)*

Row 9: Ch1 (does not count as sc throughout), turn, 3sc, 3hdc, 3dc, 2tr, 2tr in next st, ch2, 2tr in next st, 2tr, 3dc, 3hdc, 3sc. *(26 sts, one 2-ch sp)*

Row 10: Ch1, turn, 4sc, 3hdc, 3dc, 3tr, (2tr, ch2, 2tr) in 2-ch sp, 3tr, 3dc, 3hdc, 4sc. *(30 sts, one 2-ch sp)*

Row 11: Ch3, turn, 1dc in same st, 1dc in each st to corner sp, (2dc, ch2, 2dc) in corner sp, 1dc in each st to last st, 2dc in last st. *(36 sts, one 2-ch sp)*

Row 12: Ch3, turn, 1dc in each st to corner sp, (2dc, ch2, 2dc) in corner sp, 1dc in each st to end. *(40 dc, one 2-ch sp)*

Fasten off C, join A in bottom right (RS facing) corner ch sp.

Row 13: (Ch3, 2dc, ch2, 3dc) in corner sp, *[miss 2 sts, 3dc in next st] 6 times, miss 2 sts, (3dc, ch2, 3dc) in next corner sp; rep from * once more, work six 3dc groups evenly spaced in row ends of next two sides of square working (3dc, ch2, 3dc) in corner sp, slst in top of beg 3-ch to join.

Fasten off and sew in ends.

RAIN CLOUD SQUARE

(make 2)

Using A, make a magic ring.

Round 1: Ch3 (counts as 1dc throughout), 2dc in ring, [ch2, 3dc] 3 times in ring, ch2, slst in top of beg 3-ch to join. *(12 dc, four 2-ch sp)*

Round 2: Ch3, 2dc, *(2dc, ch2, 2dc) in corner sp, 1dc in each st to next corner sp; rep from * twice more, (2dc, ch2, 2dc) in next corner sp, slst in top of beg 3-ch to join. *(28 dc, four 2-ch sp)*

Round 3: Ch3, 1dc in each st to next corner sp, *(2dc, ch2, 2dc) in corner sp, 1dc in each st to next corner; rep from * twice more, (2dc, ch2, 2dc) in last corner sp, 1dc in each st to end, slst in top of beg 3-ch to join. *(44 dc, four 2-ch sp)*

Round 4: Rep Round 3. *(60 dc, four 2-ch sp)*

Round 5: Rep Round 3. *(76 dc, four 2-ch sp)*

Round 6: Ch1, 1sc in each st to next corner sp, *(1sc, ch2) in corner sp, 1sc in each st to next corner; rep from * twice more, (1sc, ch2) in last corner sp, 1sc in each st to end, slst in first sc to join. *(80 sts, four 2-ch sp)*

Fasten off A, join D in any corner sp

Round 7: (Ch3, 2dc, ch2, 3dc) in corner sp, *[miss 2 sts, 3dc in next st] 6 times, miss 2 sts, (3dc, ch2, 3dc) in corner sp; rep from * twice more, [miss 2 sts, 3dc in next st] 6 times, miss 2 sts, slst in top of beg 3-ch to join.

Fasten off and sew in ends.

CLOUD

(make 2)

Using C, ch13.

Round 1: 1sc in second ch from hook, 10sc, 3sc in the last ch, working along opp side of foundation chain, 10sc, 2sc in last ch, slst in first sc to join. *(26 sc)*

Row 2: Ch1, miss first st, 4dc in next st, 8dc, 4dc in next st, slst in next st, turn. *(16 dc)*

Row 3: Slst in next 4 dc, miss next st, 6dc in next st, miss next st, slst in next st, miss next 2 sts, (4tr, 4dc) in next st, miss next st, slst in next st.

Fasten off leaving a long tail to sew cloud to square.

RAINDROPS

(make 1 in each of B, D, E, F)

Make a magic ring.

Round 1: Ch1, 2sc in ring, ch3, 3sc in ring, slst in first sc.

Fasten off, leaving a long tail to sew raindrops to square.

FLOWER SQUARE

(make 5)

Using E, make a magic ring.

Round 1: Ch3 (counts as 1dc throughout), 11dc in ring, slst in top of beg 3-ch to join. *(12 dc)*

Round 2: Ch3, 1dc in same st, [2dc in next st] 11 times, slst in top of beg 3-ch to join. *(24 dc)*

Fasten off E, join F between any 2 dc.

Round 3: Ch1, working between dc throughout, [1sc, ch4, miss 3dc] 8 times, slst in first sc to join.

Round 4: *(Slst , ch3, 3tr, ch3, slst) in 4-ch sp, rep from * 7 times.

Fasten off F, join D into BLO of any dc from Round 2.

Round 5: Working into BLO of dc in Round 2, ch3, 2dc in next st, [1dc, 2dc in next st] 11 times, slst in top of beg 3-ch to join. *(36 sts)*

Round 6: Ch3, (1dc, ch2, 2dc) in same st, 1dc, 1hdc, 4sc, 1hdc, 1dc, *(2dc, ch2, 2dc) in next st, 1dc, 1hdc, 4sc, 1hdc, 1dc; rep from * twice, slst in top of beg 3-ch to join. *(48 sts, four 2-ch sps)*

Round 7: Ch3, 1dc in each st and (2dc, ch2, 2dc) into each 2-ch sp to end. *(64 sts)*

Round 8: Ch3, 1dc in each st and (2dc, ch2, 2dc) in each corner sp to end. *(80 sts)*

Fasten off D, join E in any corner sp.

Round 9: (Ch3, 2dc, ch2, 3dc) in corner sp, *[miss 2 sts, 3dc in next st] 6 times, miss 2 sts, (3dc, ch2, 3dc) in corner sp; rep from * twice more, [miss 2 sts, 3dc in next st] 6 times, miss 2 sts, slst in top of beg 3-ch to join.

Fasten off and sew in ends.

CONCENTRIC STRIPES SQUARE

(make 10)

Using C, make a magic ring.

Round 1: Ch3 (counts as 1dc throughout), 2dc in ring, [ch2, 3dc] 3 times in ring, ch2, slst in top of beg 3-ch to join. *(12 dc, four 2-ch sp)*

Fasten off C, join D.

Round 2: Ch3, 2dc, *(2dc, ch2, 2dc) in corner sp, 1dc in each st to next corner sp; rep from * twice more, (2dc, ch2, 2dc) in next corner sp, slst in top of beg 3-ch to join. *(28 dc, four 2-ch sp)*

Fasten off D, join A.

und 3: Ch3, 1dc in each st to next corner sp, *(2dc, 2, 2dc) in corner sp, 1dc in each st to next corner; o from * twice more, (2dc, ch2, 2dc) in last corner sp, c in each st to end, slst in top of beg 3-ch to join. *4 dc, four 2-ch sp)*
sten off A, join E.

und 4: Rep Round 3. *(60 dc, four 2-ch sp)*
sten off E, join F.

und 5: Rep Round 3. *(76 dc, four 2-ch sp)*
sten off F, join B.

und 6: Ch1, 1sc in each st to next corner sp, *(1sc, ch2) corner sp, 1sc in each st to next corner; rep from wice more, (1sc, ch2) in last corner sp, 1sc in each to end, slst in first sc to join. *(80 sts, four 2-ch sp)*

und 7: (Ch3, 2dc, ch2, 3dc) in corner sp, *[miss 2 sts, c in next st] 6 times, miss 2 sts, (3dc, ch2, 3dc) in rner sp; rep from * twice more, [miss 2 sts, 3dc in next 6 times, miss 2 sts, slst in top of beg 3-ch to join.
sten off and sew in ends.

RDER TO EACH SQUARE
in G in any corner sp.

und 1: Ch3, (2dc, ch2, 3dc) in corner sp, [3dc between xt two 3dc groups] 7 times, *(3dc, ch2, 3dc) in corner , [3dc between next two 3dc groups] 7 times; rep m * twice more, slst in top of beg 3-ch to join.
sten off.

FINISHING

Sew the cloud and the raindrops to the rain cloud square, following the photograph as a guide.
Lay out all squares in order, following the diagram as a guide. Using G, sew squares together using mattress stitch (see page 121) through the back loops only.

Main border
Worked in half double crochet over 7 rows. Work all rows in same way, changing color at end of each row in following color sequence: G, C, D, A, E, F, B.

Rows 1–7: Ch2 (counts as 1 hdc), 1hdc in each st around and (2hdc, ch2, 2hdc) in each corner sp.
Fasten off and sew in ends.

table runner

Create a unique table setting with this colorful and simple granny-square pattern. Made in variety of bright shades of durable cotton-blend yarn, this runner will protect your table from warm dishes and mugs.

SQUARE

(make 14 in A, 2 each in B, C, D, E, F, G, H)

Make a magic ring.

Round 1: Ch3 (counts as 1dc throughout), (2dc, ch2) in ring, [3dc, ch2] 3 times in ring, sl st in third ch of beg ch to join.

Round 2: Ch3, [(3dc, ch2, 3dc) in next 2-ch sp] 3 times, (3dc, ch2, 2dc) in last 2-ch sp, sl st in third ch of beg ch to join.

Round 3: Ch3, 2dc in first sp between two 3dc groups, *(3dc, ch2, 3dc) in next 2-ch sp (corner), 3dc in sp between next two 3dc groups; rep from * twice, (3dc, ch2, 3dc) in next 2-ch sp (corner), sl st in third ch of beg ch to join.

Round 4: Ch3, 3dc in sp between next two 3dc groups, *(3dc, 2ch, 3dc) in corner sp, [3dc in sp between next two 3dc groups] twice; rep from * twice, (3dc, 2ch, 3dc) in corner sp, 2dc in sp between next two 3dc groups, sl st in third ch of beg ch to join.

FINISHING

Arrange squares as you wish or use photo as guide.
Join squares together using relevant color.

BORDER

Join A to any corner.

Round 1: *(1sc, ch2, 2sc) in first corner ch sp of this side, 1sc in each st and each inner corner ch sp along this side, rep from * 3 times, sl st in first st to join. (29 sts on each short side, 197 sts on each long side)
Fasten off A, join C in any corner sp.

Round 2: *(1sc, ch2, 1sc) in corner sp, (ch3, miss 2 sc, 1sc) along this side to last 2 sc, ch3, miss 2 sc, rep from * 3 times, sl st in first st to join.
Fasten off C, join D in any corner sp.

Round 3: (2sc, ch1, 2sc) in each corner sp and 4sc in each ch sp from prev round, sl st in first st to join.
Fasten off and sew in ends (see page 120).

SKILL RATING ● ○ ○

YARN AND MATERIALS

Knitcraft Cotton Blend DK (50% cotton, 50% acrylic) light worsted (DK) weight yarn, 235yd (215m) per 3½oz (100g) ball

1 ball in each of:
Bright Blue 1005 (A)
Red 6230001001 (B)
Mustard 1001 (C)
Hot Pink 1003 (D)
Teal 1002 (E)
Yellow 1008 (F)
Lilac 6230001006 (G)
Coral 6230001007 (H)

HOOK AND EQUIPMENT

US size G/6 (4mm) crochet hook
Yarn needle

FINISHED MEASUREMENTS

Each square: 4¼in (10.5cm) square
Runner: 59in (150cm) long

ABBREVIATIONS

See page 126.

NOTE

Either use the Join-as-you-go method (see page 122) in the spaces between 3-dc groups as you work Round 4 or sew together with mattress stitch (see page 121) afterward.

tissue box cover

titch up this fun geometric design to customize an ordinary tissue
ox. Deceptively easy to make, the pattern is worked up in half-
ouble-crochet stitches in two different yarn colors. A simple
ower is crocheted and sewn onto the cover to finish.

SKILL RATING ● ● ●

ARN AND MATERIALS
omen's Institute Premium Acrylic Yarn
00% acrylic) light worsted (DK) weight
rn, 273yd (250m) per 3½oz (100g) ball
1 ball in each of:
White 1000 (A)
Orange 1002 (B)
Magenta 1031 (C)
Soft Blue 1025 (D)
ssue box 4¾in (12cm) square

OOK AND EQUIPMENT
S size G/6 (4mm) crochet hook
rn needle

NISHED MEASUREMENTS
pprox 4¾in (12cm) square

BBREVIATIONS
e page 126.

COVER SIDES
Using A, ch72, slst in first ch to form a ring.
Join B, carry yarn not in use throughout.
Round 1: Ch2, (does not count as a st throughout), [3hdc in A,
3hdc in B] 12 times, slst in first st to join. *(72 hdc)*
Round 2: Rep Round 1.
Round 3: Ch2, [3hdc in B, 3hdc in A] 12 times, slst in first st to join.
Round 4: Rep Round 3.
Rounds 5-12: Rep Rounds 1–4 twice.
Fasten off and sew in ends (see page 120).

COVER TOP
Using B, ch19.
Row 1: 1hdc in second ch from hook, 1hdc in each ch to end,
ch1, turn. *(18 hdc)*
Rows 2–5: Ch2, (does not count as a st throughout), 1hdc in each
st to end, ch1, turn.
Row 6: Ch2, 6hdc, fasten off, miss 6 sts, rejoin yarn, 1hdc in last
6 sts, ch1, turn.
Row 7: Ch2, 6hdc, ch6, 6hdc, ch1, turn.
Row 8: Ch2, 6hdc, 6hdc in 6-ch sp, 6hdc. *(18 hdc)*
Rows 9–12: 1hdc in each st to end, ch1, turn.
Fasten off leaving a long tail.

FLOWER
Using C, make a magic ring.
Round 1: 12dc into ring.
Fasten off C, join D.
Round 2: *(Slst, ch3, 2tr, ch3, slst) in next st, slst in next st;
rep from * 5 more times, slst in first slst to join.
Fasten off leaving a long tail to sew to tissue box.

FINISHING
Sew top into top edge of sides.
Sew flower onto one side of tissue box.

CHAPTER 2
Cute Gifts

With a sweet bumble bee, a mini mushroom, and bright flowers, these eye-catching bookmarks are perfect for using up colorful yarns. Each piece is quick to hook up, making this an ideal project to pick up when you have a spare moment during a busy day. One of these paired with a book would make a great gift.

bookmarks

SKILL RATING ● ● ○

YARN AND MATERIALS
Rico Ricorumi DK (100% cotton) light worsted (DK) weight yarn, 64yd (58m) per 1oz (25g) ball

For Mushroom and Star bookmark:
  1 ball in each of:
  Fuchsia 014 (A)
  White 001 (B)
  Yellow 006 (C)
  Green 049 (D)

For Flower and Leaf bookmark:
  1 ball in each of:
  Yellow 006 (C)
  Blue 032 (E)
  Green 049 (D)

For Bee and Flower bookmark:
  1 ball in each of:
  Yellow 006 (C)
  Chocolate 057 (F)
  White 001 (B)
  Green 049 (D)
  Red 028 (G)

Fabric glue if required

HOOK AND EQUIPMENT
US size C/2-D/3 (3mm) crochet hook
Yarn needle

FINISHED MEASUREMENT
Mushroom and star bookmark:
12¼in (31cm)
Flower and leaf bookmark:
12¼in (31cm)
Bee and flower bookmark:
11in (28cm)

ABBREVIATIONS
See page 126.

SPECIAL ABBREVIATION
Picot: Ch3, slst in second ch from hook, slst in next ch.

MUSHROOM AND STAR BOOKMARK
MUSHROOM CAP
Using A, make a magic ring.
Round 1: 6sc in magic ring. (6 sc)
Round 2: [2sc in next st] 6 times. (12 sc)
Round 3: 1sc in each st around.
Round 4: [1sc, 2sc in next st] 6 times. (18 sc)
Rounds 5-8: 1sc in each st around.
Fasten off and sew in ends (see page 120).

SPOTS
(make 4)
Using B, make a magic ring.
Round 1: 6sc in magic ring. (6 sc)
Fasten off, leaving long tail to sew to cap.

STALK
Using B, make a magic ring.
Round 1: 6sc in magic ring. (6 sc)
Round 2: [2sc in next st] 6 times. (12 sc)
Rounds 3-12: 1sc in each st around.
Start to stuff with fiber filling.
Round 13: [Sc2tog] 6 times. (6 sc)
Fasten off and sew in ends.

STAR
(make 2)
Using C, make a magic ring.
Round 1: Ch3 (counts as 1dc), 9dc in magic ring. *(10 dc)*
Round 2: *Ch5, 1sc in second ch from hook, 1hdc, 1dc, 1tr (point), slst in each of next 2 dc; rep from * 4 more times, ending with slst in first dc.
Fasten off leaving long tail to sew flowers together.

CORD
Using D, ch51.
Round 1: Slst in second ch from hook, slst in each st to end. *(50 slst)*
Fasten off.

FINISHING
Sew or glue both sides of star together. Sew spots onto cap, then sew cap onto stalk. Sew one end of cord to bottom of mushroom and other end between points of star. Sew in all ends.

FLOWER AND LEAF BOOKMARK
FLOWER
(make 2)
Using C, make a magic ring.
Round 1: 6sc in magic ring. *(6 sc)*
Round 2: [2sc in next st] 6 times. *(12 sc)*
Fasten off C, join E.
Round 3: *(1sc, ch2, 2tr, ch2, 1sc) in next sc, slst in next sc; rep from * 5 more times.
Fasten off leaving long tail to sew flowers together.

LEAF
(make 2)
Using D, ch9.
Round 1: 1sc in second ch from hook, 3hdc, 3dc in next ch, 2hdc, (2hdc, picot, 2hdc) in last ch, working along opp side of chain, 2hdc, 3dc in next ch, 3hdc, 1sc.
Fasten off leaving long tail to sew to cord.

CORD
Using D, ch51.
Round 1: Slst in second ch from hook, slst in each ch to end. *(50 slst)*
Fasten off.

FINISHING
Sew or glue flowers wrong sides together, sandwiching one end of cord between layers. Sew or glue leaves wrong sides together to other end of cord. Sew in all ends.

BEE AND FLOWER BOOKMARK
BEE BODY
Using C, make a magic ring.
Round 1: 6sc in magic ring. *(6 sc)*
Round 2: [2sc in next st] 6 times. *(12 sc)*
Round 3: 1sc in each st around.
Change to F, do not fasten off C.
Rounds 4 and 5: 1sc in each st around.
Change to C, do not fasten off F.
Rounds 6 and 7: 1sc in each st around.
Change to F, do not fasten off C.
Start to stuff with fiber filling.
Rounds 8 and 9: 1sc in each st around.
Change to C, fasten off F.
Round 10: 1sc in each st around.
Round 11: [Sc2tog] 6 times. *(6 sc)*
Finish stuffing, fasten off and sew closed, sew in ends.

WINGS
Using B, make a magic ring.
Round 1: (1sc, ch2, 2tr, ch2, 1sc, ch2, 2tr, ch2, slst) in magic ring.
Fasten off leaving long tail to sew to body.

FLOWER
(make 2)
Using D, make a magic ring.
Round 1: 5sc in magic ring. *(5 sc)*
Fasten off D, join G.
Round 2: [Ch3, 2dc, ch3, slst] 5 times in magic ring.
Fasten off and sew in ends.

FINISHING
Sew or glue flowers wrong sides together. Sew wings o[n] back of bee. Sew one end of cord to bottom of bee an[d] other between two petals of flower. Sew in all ends.

peg dolls

With cute mushroom hats, these little dolls would make lovely toys or decorations for a child's bedroom. You could also use them as colorful accents in your home, dotted around on shelves or on a table.

ARN AND MATERIALS
co Ricorumi DK (100% cotton) light
orsted (DK) weight yarn, 64yd (58m)
r 1oz (25g) ball
1 ball in each of:
Red 028 (A)
White 001 (B)
Candy Pink 012 (C)
Berry 015 (dark pink) (D)
Pea 077 (light green) (Vest 1)
Burgundy 030 (Vest 1)
Aqua 074 (blue) (Vest 2)
Fox 025 (orange) (Vest 2)
Nougat 056 (light brown) (Vest 3)
Mustard 064 (Vest 3)
wooden peg dolls, 1¼in (3.5cm) diameter
4¾in (12cm) tall
bric glue

OOK AND EQUIPMENT
size C/2-D/3 (3mm) crochet hook
rn needle

NISHED MEASUREMENTS
in (3.5cm) diameter x 4¾in (12cm) tall

BBREVIATIONS
 e page 126.

LARGE MUSHROOM TOP
OUTER RED CAP
Using A, make a magic ring.
Round 1: 6sc in magic ring. *(6 sc)*
Round 2: [2sc in next st] 6 times. *(12 sc)*
Round 3: [1sc, 2sc in next st] 6 times. *(18 sc)*
Round 4: [2sc, 2sc in next st] 6 times. *(24 sc)*
Round 5: [3sc, 2sc in next st] 6 times. *(30 sc)*
Round 6: [4sc, 2sc in next st] 6 times. *(36 sc)*
Round 7: [5sc, 2sc in next st] 6 times. *(42 sc)*
Rounds 8 to 10: 1sc in each st around.
Do not fasten off.

INNER WHITE CAP
Using B, make a magic ring.
Rounds 1-7: Rep Rounds 1-7 of outer red cap.
Rounds 8 and 9: 1sc in each st around.
Fasten off and sew in ends.
Put B cap inside A cap, using A work 1sc through both parts of cap in each st around. *(42 sc)*
Fasten off and sew in ends (see page 120).

MEDIUM MUSHROOM TOP
OUTER PINK CAP
Using C, make a magic ring.
Round 1: 6sc in magic ring. *(6 sc)*
Round 2: 1sc in each st around.
Round 3: [2sc in next st] 6 times. *(12 sc)*
Round 4: 1sc in each st around.
Round 5: [1sc, 2sc in next st] 6 times. *(18 sc)*
Round 6: 1sc in each st around.
Round 7: [2sc, 2sc in next st] 6 times. *(24 sc)*
Round 8: 1sc in each st around.
Round 9: [3sc, 2sc in next st] 6 times. *(30 sc)*
Round 10: 1sc in each st around.
Round 11: [4sc, 2sc in next st] 6 times. *(36 sc)*
Round 12: 1sc in each st around.
Round 13: [5sc, 2sc in next st] 6 times. *(42 sc)*
Do not fasten off.

INNER WHITE CAP
Using B, make a magic ring.
Rounds 1–13: Rep Rounds 1–13 of outer pink cap.
Put B cap inside C cap, using C work 1sc through both parts of cap in each st around. *(42 sc)*

SMALL MUSHROOM TOP
OUTER BERRY CAP
Using D, make a magic ring.
Round 1: 6sc in magic ring. *(6 sc)*
Round 2: [2sc in next st] 6 times. *(12 sc)*
Round 3: [1sc, 2sc in next st] 6 times. *(18 sc)*
Round 4: [2sc, 2sc in next st] 6 times. *(24 sc)*

Round 5: [3sc, 2sc in next st] 6 times. *(30 sc)*
Rounds 6–8: 1sc in each st around.
Do not fasten off.

INNER WHITE CAP
Using B, make a magic ring.
Rounds 1–5: Rep Rounds 1–5 of outer berry cap.
Rounds 6 and 7: 1sc in each st around.
Fasten off and sew in ends.
Put B cap inside D cap, using D work 1sc through both parts of cap in each st around. *(30 sc)*

SMALL SPOTS
(make 13)
Using B, make a magic ring.
Round 1: 6sc in magic ring. *(6 sc)*
Fasten off leaving long end to sew to cap.

BIG SPOTS
(make 6)
Using B, make a magic ring.
Round 1: 6sc in magic ring. *(6 sc)*
Round 2: [2sc in next st] 6 times. *(12 sc)*
Fasten off leaving long end to sew to cap.

VEST
(make 3)
For Vest 1 change color every 2 rows, for Vest 2 every 3 rows, for Vest 3 work half and half.
Using first color, ch22, slst in first ch to form a ring.
Work in continuous rounds.
Rounds 1–14: 1sc in each st around. *(22 sc)*
Fasten off and sew in ends.

FINISHING
Sew 3 big spots and 4 small spots on large mushroom cap.
Sew 2 big spots and 5 small spots on medium mushroom cap.
Sew 1 big spot and 4 small spots on small mushroom cap.
Glue each cap to a wooden doll.
Dress each wooden doll in a vest.

lavender heart

Embellished with a mini crocheted flower and leaves, this lavender heart would make a perfect gift or stocking filler. Put the heart on a coat hanger in a wardrobe or tuck it into a drawer to keep clothes smelling floral and fresh. Hanging up in a room, it doubles up as a beautiful decoration.

SKILL RATING ● ● ○

YARN AND MATERIALS
Women's Institute Premium Acrylic Yarn (100% acrylic) light worsted (DK) weight yarn, 273yd (250m) per 3½oz (100g) ball
1 ball in each of:
    Red (A)
    Soft Pink (B)
    Yellow (C)
    Green (D)
    Soft Blue (E)
Lavender bag
Small amount of fiber filling

HOOK AND EQUIPMENT
US size G/6 (4mm) hook
Yarn needle

FINISHED MEASUREMENTS
5in (13cm) wide x 4¼in (11cm) tall

ABBREVIATIONS
See page 126.

SPECIAL ABBREVIATION
PC (popcorn): work 6dc all in one st, remove live loop from hook, insert hook in top of first dc, place loop on hook and pull through.

HEART
FRONT AND BACK
(make 2)
Using A, make a magic ring.
Round 1: Ch2, 11dc in magic ring, slst in second ch of beg ch. *(11 dc, ch-2)*
Round 2: Ch2, [2dc in next dc] 11 times, slst in second ch of beg ch. *(22 dc, ch-2)*
Round 3: Ch2, [2dc in next dc, 1dc] 5 times, 2dc in next dc, 3dc in next dc, [1dc, 2dc in next dc] 5 times, slst in second ch of beg ch. *(35 dc, ch-2)*
Round 4: 1sc in top of ch-2, (1hdc, 1dc) in next dc, [2dc in next dc] 5 times, 2dc, 2hdc, 4sc, 1hdc, 1dc, 3dc in next dc, 1dc, 1hdc, 4sc, 2hdc, 2dc, [2dc in next dc] 5 times, (1dc, 1hdc) in next dc, 1sc, slst in first st. *(10 sc, 8 hdc, 31 dc, 1 slst)*
Round 5: Slst in first sc, 1sc, 1hdc, (1hdc, 1dc) in next st, [2dc in next st] 6 times, 3dc, 2hdc, 19sc, 2hdc, 3dc, [2dc in next st] 6 times, (1dc, 1hdc) in next st, 1hdc, 1sc, slst, slst in first st *(21 sc, 8 hdc, 32 dc, 3 slst)*
Fasten off and sew in ends (see page 120).

FLOWER
Using B, make a magic ring.
Round 1: Ch2 (counts as 1hdc), 5hdc, slst in second ch of beg ch. *(6 hdc)*
Fasten off B, join C.
Round 2: PC in each sp between hdc. *(6 PC)*
Fasten off C leaving long tail to sew to front of heart.

LEAF
(make 2)
Using D, ch7.
Round 1: 1sc in second ch from hook, 1hdc, 2dc in next ch, 1hdc, 1sc, 3sc in last ch, working along opp side of chain, 1sc, 1hdc, 2dc in next ch, 1hdc, 1sc, slst in first st.

...sten off leaving long tail to sew to underside of flower.

...ANGING LOOP
...sing D, ch21, leaving a long tail.
...w 1: 1sc in second ch from hook, 1sc in each
...maining ch. *(20 sc)*
...sten off leaving long tail to sew to top of heart.

...NISHING
...t both hearts WS tog, join using E, with slst around
...oth hearts (see page 122), placing dried lavender
...g and small amount fiber filling inside before
...mpleting seam. *(64 slst)*
...w flower and leaves to front of heart. Sew both
...ds of hanging loop to top center of heart.

mug cozy

Keep your cup of coffee warm with this sweet floral cozy. Quick to make, the pattern is made up of three simple granny squares which are sewn together and finished with a border, button loop, and button. Why not stitch up a set of these in different colors for your mug collection?

SKILL RATING ● ○ ○

YARN AND MATERIALS
Rico Ricorumi DK (100% cotton) light
worsted (DK) weight yarn, 64yd (58m)
per 1oz (25g) ball
1 ball in each of:
Yellow 006 (A)
Berry 015 (bright pink) (B)
Green 049 (C)
Yellow button

HOOK AND EQUIPMENT
US size E/4 (3.5mm) crochet hook
Yarn needle

FINISHED MEASUREMENTS
13in (33cm) circumference,
3¼in (8.5cm) tall

ABBREVIATIONS
See page 126.

SPECIAL ABBREVIATION
3dcCL (three-double-crochet cluster):
yoh, insert hook in st, yoh, pull through
2 loops on hook), yoh, pull through first
2 loops on hook (2 loops on hook), yoh,
insert hook in same st, yoh, pull through
2 loops on hook), yoh, pull through first
2 loops on hook (3 loops on hook), yoh,
insert hook in same st, yoh, pull through
2 loops on hook), yoh, pull through first
2 loops on hook (4 loops on hook), yoh,
pull through all 4 loops on hook.

COZY
SQUARES
(make 3)
Using A, make a magic ring.
Round 1: Working in magic ring, ch4 (counts as 1dc, ch1), [1dc, ch1] 7 times. *(8 dc, 8ch sps)*
Fasten off A, join B.
Round 2: Working in ch sps, [3dcCL, ch2] 8 times.
Fasten off B, join C.
Round 3: Working in ch sps, ch3 (counts as 1dc), (2dc, ch2, 3dc) in same ch sp to make corner, 3sc in next ch sp, *(3dc, ch2, 3dc) in next ch sp to make corner, 3sc in next ch sp; rep from * 2 more times, slst in third ch of beg ch.
Round 4: Working in ch sps, ch3 (counts as 1dc), (2dc, ch2, 3dc) in same ch sp to make corner, 3sc in next 2 ch sps, *(3dc, ch2, 3dc) in corner ch sp, 3dc in next 2 ch sps; rep from * 2 more times, slst in third ch of beg ch.
Fasten off.

FINISHING
Sew squares together into a strip, then work 1sc in each st around, working 3sc in each corner.
Join last two sides together for ⅜in (1cm) up from bottom to make a ring, leaving rest of sides open above.
At top of opening, sew on button.
Button loop
Join C on side opposite button, ch11.
Row 1: Slst in second ch from hook, 9slst to end.
Fasten off leaving a long tail to sew other end of chain down to make button loop.

refrigerator magnet

This is a fun and simple project to start with if you are new to crochet. Made in brightly colored cotton yarn, the mini crocheted pieces make super-cute magnets for a refrigerator or you could even sew them onto a bag or jacket.

SKILL RATING ● ● ●

YARN AND MATERIALS
Rico Ricorumi DK (100% cotton) light worsted (DK) weight yarn, 64yd (58m) per 1oz (25g) ball
  1 ball in each of:
  Sky Blue 031 (A)
  Green 049 (B)
  Yellow 006 (C)
  Orange 027 (D)
  Red 028 (E)
  Fuchsia 014 (F)
  Tangerine 026 (G)
  White 001 (H)
5 small round magnets

HOOK AND EQUIPMENT
US size E/4 (3.5mm) crochet hook
Yarn needle
Fabric glue

FINISHED MEASUREMENTS
Rainbow: 2¾in (7cm) across
Sunshine: 3¼in (8cm) across
Flower: 2½in (6.5cm) across
Strawberry: 1¾in (4.5cm) across
Mushroom: 2½in (6.5cm) across

ABBREVIATIONS
See page 126.

SPECIAL ABBREVIATION
Picot: Ch3, slst in second ch from hook, slst in next ch.

RAINBOW
Using A, ch4.
Row 1: 1sc in second ch from hook, 1sc, 3sc in last ch, working along opp side of chain, 2sc. *(7 sts)*
Fasten off A, join B in first sc of Row 1.
Row 2: Ch1 (does not count as st throughout), 2sc, [2sc in next st] 3 times, 2sc. *(10 sts)*
Fasten off B, join C in first sc of Row 2.
Row 3: Ch1, 2sc, [1sc, 2sc in next st] 3 times, 2sc. *(13 sts)*
Fasten off C, join D in first sc of Row 3.
Row 4: Ch1, 2sc, [2sc, 2sc in next st] 3 times, 2sc. *(16 sts)*
Fasten off D, join E in first sc of Row 4.
Row 5: Ch1, 2sc, [3sc, 2sc in next st] 3 times, 2sc. *(19 sts)*
Fasten off E, join F in first sc of Row 5.
Row 6: Ch1, 2sc, [4sc, 2sc in next st] 3 times, 2sc. *(22 sts)*
Fasten off.

SUNSHINE
Using C, make a magic ring.
Round 1: 6sc in magic ring. *(6 sts)*
Round 2: [2sc in next st] 6 times. *(12 sts)*
Round 3: [1sc, 2sc in next st] 6 times. *(18 sts)*
Round 4: [2sc, 2sc in next st] 6 times. *(24 sts)*
Round 5: [3sc, 2sc in next st] 6 times. *(30 sts)*
Fasten off C, join G to any st.
Round 6: *(1sc, 1dc, picot) in next st, (1dc, 1sc) in next st; rep from * 14 more times.
Fasten off.

MUSHROOM

Using E, make a magic ring.
Row 1: 3sc in magic ring, ch1, turn.
(3 sts)
Row 2: [2sc in next st] 3 times, ch1, turn. *(6 sts)*
Row 3: [1sc, 2sc in next st] 3 times, ch1, turn. *(9 sts)*
Row 4: [2sc, 2sc in next st] 3 times, ch1, turn. *(12 sts)*
Row 5: [3sc, 2sc in next st] 3 times, ch1, turn. *(15 sts)*
Row 6: 1sc in each st.
Fasten off.

STALK

Using H, ch4.
Row 1: 1sc in second ch from hook, 1sc, 3sc in last ch, working along opp side of chain, 2sc, turn. *(7 sts)*
Row 2: Ch1 (does not count as st), 2sc, [2sc in next st] 3 times, 2sc, turn. *(10 sts)*
Fasten off.

SPOT

(make 3)
Using H, make a magic ring.
Round 1: 6sc in magic ring. *(6 sts)*
Fasten off.

FINISHING

Sew in ends (see page 120) on Rainbow, Sunshine, and Flower and glue a magnetic disc to back of each.
For Strawberry, sew on stalk, sew in ends, and glue a magnetic disc to back.
For Mushroom, sew spots to cap, sew stalk to cap, then sew in ends. Glue a magnetic disc to back.

FLOWER

Using F, make a magic ring.
Round 1: 6sc in magic ring. *(6 sts)*
Round 2: [2sc in next st] 6 times. *(12 sts)*
Round 3: [1sc, 2sc in next st] 6 times. *(18 sc)*
Fasten off F, join D to any st.
Round 4: *(Slst, 1dc, 1tr) in next st, (1tr, 1dc, slst) in next st, slst; rep from * 5 more times.
Fasten off.

STRAWBERRY

Using E, make a magic ring.
Round 1: Ch3 (counts as first dc), 11dc in magic ring. *(12 sts)*
Round 2: (1hdc, 1dc) in first st, 3dc in next st, 2hdc, 3hdc in next st, 2hdc, 3dc in next st, (1dc, 1hdc) in next st, 1sc, slst, 1sc. *(20 sts)*
Fasten off.

STALK

Using B.
Row 1: [Ch3, 1sc in second ch from hook, 1sc] 3 times.
Fasten off.

Coasters are always useful for any home, and this playful set would make a lovely gift. The spots on the ladybug's wings are crocheted separately and then stitched on. You could make several of the flower designs with different colors for the petals.

ladybug and flower coasters

SKILL RATING ● ○ ○

YARN AND MATERIALS
Rico Ricorumi DK (100% cotton)
light worsted (DK) weight yarn,
64yd (58m) per 1oz (25g) ball
For the Ladybug coasters
   1 ball in each of:
   Red 028 (A)
   Black 060 (B)
For the Flower coasters
   1 ball in each of:
   Yellow 006 (C)
   Orchid 016 (pink) (D)

HOOK AND EQUIPMENT
US size E/4 (3.5mm) crochet hook

Yarn needle

FINISHED MEASUREMENTS
Ladybug coaster: 4¾in
(12cm) across

Flower coaster: 5in (13cm) across

ABBREVIATIONS
See page 126.

LADYBUG
BODY
Using A, make a magic ring.
Round 1: 6sc in magic ring. *(6 sts)*
Round 2: [2sc in next st] 6 times. *(12 sts)*
Round 3: [1sc, 2sc in next st] 6 times. *(18 sts)*
Round 4: [2sc, 2sc in next st] 6 times. *(24 sts)*
Round 5: [3sc, 2sc in next st] 6 times. *(30 sts)*
Round 6: [4sc, 2sc in next st] 6 times. *(36 sts)*
Round 7: [5sc, 2sc in next st] 6 times. *(42 sts)*
Round 8: [6sc, 2sc in next st] 6 times. *(48 sts)*
Round 9: [7sc, 2sc in next st] 6 times. *(54 sts)*
Round 10: [8sc, 2sc in next st] 6 times. *(60 sts)*
Round 11: [9sc, 2sc in next st] 6 times. *(66 sts)*
Round 12: [10sc, 2sc in next st] 6 times. *(72 sts)*
Fasten off A and join B.
Round 13: Slst in each st around, then slst across diameter
over each round to create line to divide wings.
Fasten off and sew in ends (see page 120).

HEAD

Using B, make a magic ring.
Row 1: 3sc in magic ring, ch1, turn. *(3 sts)*
Row 2: [2sc in next st] 3 times, ch1, turn. *(6 sts)*
Row 3: [1sc, 2sc in next st] 3 times, ch1, turn. *(9 sts)*
Row 4: [2sc, 2sc in next st] 3 times, ch1, turn. *(12 sts)*
Row 5: [3sc, 2sc in next st] 3 times. *(15 sts)*
Fasten off and sew in ends.

SPOTS

(make 6)
Using B, make a magic ring.
Round 1: 6sc in magic ring. *(6 sts)*
Round 2: [2sc in next st] 6 times. *(12 sts)*
Fasten off.

FLOWER

Using C, make a magic ring.
Round 1: 6sc in magic ring. *(6 sts)*
Round 2: [2sc in next st] 6 times. *(12 sts)*
Round 3: [1sc, 2sc in next st] 6 times. *(18 sts)*
Round 4: [2sc, 2sc in next st] 6 times. *(24 sts)*
Round 5: [3sc, 2sc in next st] 6 times. *(30 sts)*
Round 6: [4sc, 2sc in next st] 6 times. *(36 sts)*
Round 7: [5sc, 2sc in next st] 6 times. *(42 sts)*
Round 8: [6sc, 2sc in next st] 6 times. *(48 sts)*
Round 9: [7sc, 2sc in next st] 6 times. *(54 sts)*
Round 10: [8sc, 2sc in next st] 6 times. *(60 sts)*
Fasten off C and join D.
Round 11: *Slst, (ch3, 1tr) in next st, 2tr in next st, (1tr, ch3, slst) in next st; rep from * 14 more times to create 15 petals.

FINISHING

Sew spots onto ladybug.

This adorable hot water bottle cover is sure to bring a smile to a loved one's face. The main cover is made up of simple blocks of color, and the door and windows are crocheted separately and sewn on. Window boxes complete with tiny flowers are added to finish.

little house hot water bottle cover

SKILL RATING ● ● ◐

YARN AND MATERIALS
Women's Institute Premium Acrylic Yarn (100% acrylic) light worsted (DK) weight yarn, 273yd (250m)
  1 ball in each of:
  Soft Blue 1025 (A)
  Yellow 1005 (B)
  Green 1001 (C)
  Red 1015 (D)
  Blue 1024 (E)
  White 1000 (F)
20in (50cm) length of elastic
Hot water bottle 6¾in (17cm) wide

HOOK AND EQUIPMENT
US size G/6 (4mm) crochet hook

Yarn needle

FINISHED MEASUREMENTS
7in (18cm) wide by 13in (33cm) tall with bottom folded inside

ABBREVIATIONS
See page 126.

COVER
Using A, ch60, slst in first ch to form a ring.
Work in continuous rounds throughout.
House section
Rounds 1–34: 1sc in each st around. *(60 sts)*
Fasten off A, join B.
Roof section
Round 35: 1sc in each st around.
Work in BLO for all foll rounds.
Round 36: 1sc in each st around.
Round 37: 14sc, [sc2tog], 28sc, [sc2tog], 14sc. *(58 sts)*
Round 38: 13sc, [sc2tog], 28sc, [sc2tog], 13sc. *(56 sts)*
Round 39: 13sc, [sc2tog], 26sc, [sc2tog], 13sc. *(54 sts)*
Round 40: 12sc, [sc2tog], 26sc, [sc2tog], 12sc. *(52 sts)*
Round 41: 12sc, [sc2tog], 24sc, [sc2tog], 12sc. *(50 sts)*
Round 42: 11sc, [sc2tog], 24sc, [sc2tog], 11sc. *(48 sts)*
Round 43: 11sc, [sc2tog], 22sc, [sc2tog], 11sc. *(46 sts)*
Round 44: 10sc, [sc2tog], 22sc, [sc2tog], 10sc. *(44 sts)*
Round 45: 10sc, [sc2tog], 20sc, [sc2tog], 10sc. *(42 sts)*
Round 46: 9sc, [sc2tog], 20sc, [sc2tog], 9sc. *(40 sts)*
Round 47: Work 1sc in each st around.
Fasten off leaving a long tail to sew top of roof shut.

Grass section

Join C to Round 1.

Round 1: 1sc in each foundation ch around. *(60 sts)*

Round 2: [1sc, 1dc] 30 times.

Round 3: [1dc, 1sc] 30 times.

Rounds 4–7: Rep Rounds 2 and 3 twice.

Round 8: 1sc in each st around.

Round 9: 1scBLO in each st around.

Rounds 10–15: 1sc in each st around.

Tie ends of elastic together to form a loop slightly smaller than diameter of water bottle cover.

Round 16: Working over elastic, 1sc in each st around. Fasten off and sew in ends.

DOOR

Using D, ch5.

Row 1: 1sc in second ch from hook, 3sc, ch1, turn. *(4 sts)*

Rows 2–6: 1sc in each st to end, ch1, turn.

Edging

Round 7: 1sc in each st or row end around all sides of door, working 1 extra sc in each corner sp. *(24 sts)* Fasten off leaving a long tail to sew door to house.

DOOR HANDLE

Using B, make a magic ring.

Round 1: 4sc in magic ring, slst in first sc.

Fasten off leaving a long tail to sew to door.

WINDOW

(make 4)

Using E, ch5.

Row 1: 1sc in second ch from hook, 3sc, ch1, turn. *(4 sts*

Rows 2–4: 1sc in each st to end, ch1, turn.

Fasten off E, join F.

Round 5: 1sc in each st or row end around all sides of window, working 1 extra sc in each corner sp. *(20 sts)* Fasten off leaving a long tail to sew window details and to sew window to house.

WINDOW BOX

(make 4)

Using B, ch7.

Row 1: 1sc in second ch from hook, 5sc, ch1, turn. *(6 sts* Fasten off leaving a long tail to sew to lower part of window.

FINISHING

Sew top of roof closed.

Sew door in middle at base of house. Sew on door handle.

Sew on windows and use yarn end in F to sew across middle horizontally and vertically for window bars.

Sew a window box below each window. Using D, make 4 to 5 French knots (see page 126) per window box for flowers. Using C, sew 10 to 12 straight stitches per window box for leaves.

Fold Rounds 10 to 16 of grass section inside and water bottle will sit inside neatly.

pencil toppers

Make your stationery stand out with these cute and colorful pencil toppers. If you're a beginner, these designs are a great way to practice your techniques on small-scale projects. A set of these toppers with colorful pencils would make a lovely gift for a child.

KILL RATING ● ○ ○

ARN AND MATERIALS

ico Ricorumi DK (100% cotton) light orsted (DK) weight yarn, 64yd (58m) er 1oz (25g) ball

For Mushroom Pencil Holder:
1 ball in each of:
White 001 (A)
Orchid 016 (B)

For Sunshine Pencil Holder:
1 ball in each of:
Tangerine 026 (C)
Yellow 006 (D)

For Flower Pencil Holder:
1 ball in each of:
Pistachio 047 (E)
Fuchsia 014 (F)
Sky Blue 031 (G)

mall amount of fiber filling

OOK AND EQUIPMENT
S size E/4 (3.5mm) crochet hook
arn needle

INISHED MEASUREMENTS
ushroom pencil holder: 3in (7.5cm)
unshine pencil holder: 3½in (9cm)
ower pencil holder: 3¼in (8.5cm)

BBREVIATIONS
ee page 126.

SPECIAL ABBREVIATION
Picot: Ch3, slst in second ch from hook, slst in next ch.

MUSHROOM
PENCIL HOLDER
Using A, make a magic ring.
Round 1: 6sc in magic ring. *(6 sts)*
Rounds 2–16: 1sc in each st around.
Fasten off.

CAP
Using B, make a magic ring.
Round 1: 6sc in magic ring. *(6 sts)*
Round 2: [2sc in next st] 6 times. *(12 sts)*
Round 3: [1sc, 2sc in next st] 6 times. *(18 sc)*
Rounds 4–8: 1sc in each st around. *(18 sts)*
Fasten off.

FINISHING
Using A, evenly stitch eight French knots (see page 126) around cap.
Sew in ends and sew cap to stalk.

SUNSHINE
PENCIL HOLDER
Using C, make a magic ring.
Round 1: 6sc in magic ring. *(6 sts)*
Rounds 2–10: 1sc in each st around.
Fasten off.

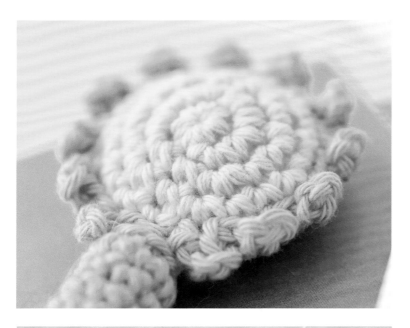

SUN
Using D, make a magic ring.
Round 1: 6sc in magic ring. *(6 sts)*
Round 2: [2sc in next st] 6 times. *(12 sts)*
Round 3: [1sc, 2sc in next st] 6 times. *(18 sc)*
Round 4: [2sc, 2sc in next st] 6 times. *(24 sc)*
Fasten off and make a second circle in D, following Rounds 1 to 4.

Sun rays
Place one circle on top of other, with RS facing out, and join using C as follows, stuffing as you go.
Round 5: [Slst, picot, slst] 12 times.
Fasten off.

FINISHING
Sew both parts of pencil topper together and sew in ends (see page 120).

FLOWER
PENCIL HOLDER
Using E, make a magic ring.
Round 1: 6sc in magic ring. *(6 sts)*
Rounds 2–10: 1sc in each st around.
Fasten off.

FLOWER
Using F, make a magic ring.
Round 1: 6sc in magic ring. *(6 sts)*
Round 2: [2sc in next st] 6 times. *(12 sts)*
Fasten off and make a second circle in F, following Rounds 1 and 2.
Place one circle on top of other, with RS facing out, and join using G as follows.
Round 3: *(Slst, ch2, 1dc) in next st, (1dc, ch2, slst) in next st; rep from * 5 more times.
Fasten off.

FINISHING
Sew both parts of pencil topper together and sew in ends.

Add a cute focal point to your bookshelf with these quirky gnome characters. The 3D shapes are made with simple single crochet stitches, and each gnome is finished with a popcorn-stitch nose and brightly colored eyes. Why not try using different yarns to make striped outfits for Mr and Mrs Gnome?

gnome sweet gnome bookends

SKILL RATING ● ● ○

YARN AND MATERIALS
Rico Ricorumi DK (100% cotton) light worsted (DK) weight yarn, 64yd (58m) per 1oz (25g) ball
  1 ball in each of:
  Red 028 (A)
  Green 044 (B)
  Beige 055 (C)
  White 001 (D)
  Pastel Yellow 062 (E)
  Tangerine 026 (F)
  Sky Blue 031 (G)
  Black (H)
2 pairs of ½in (8mm) blue or green safety eyes

Fiber filling
Wooden bookends
Glue

HOOK AND EQUIPMENT
US size E/4 (3.5mm) crochet hook
Yarn needle

FINISHED MEASUREMENTS
Each gnome on a mushroom approx. 10¼in (26cm) tall

ABBREVIATIONS
See page 126.

SPECIAL ABBREVIATION
PC (popcorn): work 6dc all in one st, remove live loop from hook, insert hook in top of first dc, place loop on hook and pull through.

NOTE
Both gnomes are made in the same way, with a hat, head, body, legs, and arms.

If you don't want to use wooden bookends, weight the base of the mushrooms before adding fiber filling and use as bookends without the wooden part.

GNOME

HAT

(make 1 in A, 1 in B)

Make a magic ring.

Round 1: 6sc in magic ring. *(6 sts)*
Round 2: 1sc in each st.
Round 3: [1sc, 2sc in next st] 3 times. *(9 sts)*
Round 4: 1sc in each st.
Round 5: [2sc, 2sc in next st] 3 times. *(12 sts)*
Round 6: 1sc in each st.
Round 7: [3sc, 2sc in next st] 3 times. *(15 sts)*
Round 8: 1sc in each st.
Round 9: [4sc, 2sc in next st] 3 times. *(18 sts)*
Round 10: 1sc in each st.
Round 11: [5sc, 2sc in next st] 3 times. *(21 sts)*
Round 12: 1sc in each st.
Round 13: [6sc, 2sc in next st] 3 times. *(24 sts)*
Round 14: 1sc in each st.
Round 15: [7sc, 2sc in next st] 3 times. *(27 sts)*
Round 16: 1sc in each st.

Fasten off leaving a long tail to sew to head.

HEAD

(make 2)

Using C, make a magic ring.

Round 1: 6sc in magic ring. *(6 sts)*
Round 2: [2sc in next st] 6 times. *(12 sts)*
Round 3: [1sc, 2sc in next st] 6 times. *(18 sts)*
Round 4: [2sc, 2sc in next st] 6 times. *(24 sts)*
Rounds 5 and 6: 1sc in each st around.
Round 7: 11sc, PC, 12sc.
Rounds 8 and 9: 1sc in each st around. *(24 sts)*

Insert safety eyes between Rounds 8 and 9, either side of nose, 5 sts apart.

Round 10: [2sc, sc2tog] 6 times. *(18 sts)*

Start to stuff with fiber filling.

Round 11: [1sc, sc2tog] 6 times. *(12 sts)*
Round 12: [sc2tog] 6 times. *(6 sts)*

Fasten off and sew gap closed.

MR GNOME'S BEARD

Using D, make a magic ring.

Row 1: 3sc in magic ring, ch1, turn. *(3 sts)*
Row 2: [2sc in next st] 3 times, ch1, turn. *(6 sts)*
Row 3: [1sc, 2sc in next st] 3 times, ch1, turn. *(9 sts)*
Row 4: [2sc, 2sc in next st] 3 times, ch1, turn. *(12 sts)*
Row 5: [3sc, 2sc in next st] 3 times, ch1, turn. *(15 sts)*
Row 6: [4sc, 2sc in next st] 3 times. *(18 sts)*

Fasten off leaving a long tail to sew to face.

MRS GNOME'S HAIR

Using E, make a magic ring.

Round 1: 6sc in magic ring. *(6 sts)*
Round 2: [2sc in next st] 6 times. *(12 sts)*
Round 3: [1sc, 2sc in next st] 6 times. *(18 sts)*
Round 4: [2sc, 2sc in next st] 6 times. *(24 sts)*
Round 5: [3sc, 2sc in next st] 6 times. *(30 sts)*
Round 6: 14sc, [ch15, slst into the second ch, sl st in next 13 ch, sl st in next st from Round 5] 16 times, slst into the first st.

Fasten off, leaving a long tail to sew to Mrs Gnome's head.

BODY

(make 2)

Using F for Mr Gnome and G for Mrs Gnome, make a magic ring.

Round 1: 6sc in magic ring. *(6 sts)*
Round 2: [2sc in next st] 6 times. *(12 sts)*
Round 3: [1sc, 2sc in next st] 6 times. *(18 sts)*
Round 4: [2sc, 2sc in next st] 6 times. *(24 sts)*
Round 5: [3sc, 2sc in next st] 6 times. *(30 sts)*
Rounds 6–9: 1sc in each st around.
Change to B for Mr Gnome only.
Round 10: 1scBLO in each st around.
Rounds 11 and 12: 1sc in each st around.
Round 13: [3sc, sc2tog] 6 times. *(24 sts)*
Round 14: [2sc, sc2tog] 6 times. *(18 sts)*
Start to stuff with fiber filling.
Round 15: [1sc, sc2tog] 6 times. *(12 sts)*
Round 16: [Sc2tog] 6 times. *(6 sts)*
Fasten off and sew gap closed.

MRS GNOME'S SKIRT
Join G to missed FLs of Round 10 of Mrs Gnome's body.
Round 1: [4sc, 2sc in next st] 6 times. *(36 sts)*
Rounds 2–9: 1sc in each st around.
Fasten off and sew in the ends.

ARM/LEG
(make 4 in C for arms, 4 in H for legs)
Make a magic ring.
Round 1: 6sc in magic ring. *(6 sts)*
Round 2: [1sc, 2sc in next st] 3 times. *(9 sts)*
Round 3: 1sc in each st around.
Start to stuff with fiber filling.
Round 4: [1sc, sc2tog] 3 times. *(6 sts)*
Arms
Change to F for Mr Gnome, change to G for Mrs Gnome.
Legs
Change to B for Mr Gnome, work 2 rounds A, 2 rounds D alternately for Mrs Gnome.
Rounds 5–12: 1sc in each st around.
Fasten off leaving a long tail to sew to body.

MUSHROOM
STALK
Using D, make a magic ring.
Round 1: 6sc in magic ring. *(6 sts)*
Round 2: [2sc in next st] 6 times. *(12 sts)*
Round 3: [1sc, 2sc in next st] 6 times. *(18 sts)*
Round 4: [2sc, 2sc in next st] 6 times. *(24 sts)*
Round 5: [3sc, 2sc in next st] 6 times. *(30 sts)*
Round 6: [4sc, 2sc in next st] 6 times. *(36 sts)*
Round 7: 1scBLO in each st around.
Rounds 8–15: 1sc in each st around.
Round 16: [5sc, 2sc in next st] 6 times. *(42 sts)*
Round 17: [6sc, 2sc in next st] 6 times. *(48 sts)*

Round 18: [7sc, 2sc in next st] 6 times. *(54 sts)*
Round 19: [8sc, 2sc in next st] 6 times. *(60 sts)*
Fasten off and sew in the ends.

CAP
(make 1 in A, 1 in F)
Make a magic ring.
Round 1: 6sc in magic ring. *(6 sts)*
Round 2: [2sc in next st] 6 times. *(12 sts)*
Round 3: [1sc, 2sc in next st] 6 times. *(18 sts)*
Round 4: [2sc, 2sc in next st] 6 times. *(24 sts)*
Round 5: [3sc, 2sc in next st] 6 times. *(30 sts)*
Round 6: [4sc, 2sc in next st] 6 times. *(36 sts)*
Round 7: [5sc, 2sc in next st] 6 times. *(42 sts)*
Round 8: [6sc, 2sc in next st] 6 times. *(48 sts)*
Round 9: [7sc, 2sc in next st] 6 times. *(54 sts)*
Round 10: [8sc, 2sc in next st] 6 times. *(60 sts)*
Rounds 11–13: 1sc in each st around.
Place cap on stalk.
Round 14: 1sc in each st around working in both cap and stalk to join, at roughly halfway around, start to stuff with fiber filling and cont to stuff until closed.

SMALL SPOTS
(make 6)
Using D, make a magic ring.
Round 1: 6sc in magic ring. *(6 sts)*
Fasten off leaving a long tail to sew to cap.

LARGE SPOTS
(make 4)
Using D, make a magic ring.
Round 1: 6sc in magic ring. *(6 sts)*
Round 2: [2sc in next st] 6 times. *(12 sts)*
Fasten off leaving a long tail to sew to cap.

FINISHING
Sew hair to Mrs Gnome's head. Sew cap onto each head, sew head to body. Sew on arms and legs. Sew beard to Mr Gnome's face and sew three small and two large spots to each mushroom cap, then sew a gnome sitting on top.
Glue each assembled gnome and mushroom onto a wooden bookend.

Super-quick to hook up and made in durable cotton yarn, this sweet keyring will help you find your keys easily. This project only needs a small amount of yarn, so it's perfect for using up scraps leftover from other projects. One of these would make a lovely housewarming gift.

mushroom home keyring

SKILL RATING ● ● ○

YARN AND MATERIALS
Rico Ricorumi DK (100% cotton) light worsted (DK) weight yarn, 64yd (58m) per 1oz (25g) ball
   1 ball in each of:
   Tangerine 026 (A)
   White 001 (B)
   Beige 055 (C)
   Sky Blue 031 (D)
   Green 049 (E)

Split ring

HOOK AND EQUIPMENT
US size E/4 (3.5mm) crochet hook

Yarn needle

FINISHED MEASUREMENTS
Mushroom: 2¾in (7cm) wide by 3¼in (8cm) high

ABBREVIATIONS
See page 126.

MUSHROOM
CAP
Using A, make a magic ring.
Round 1: 6sc in magic ring. *(6 sts)*
Round 2: [2sc in next st] 6 times. *(12 sts)*
Round 3: [1sc, 2sc in next st] 6 times. *(18 sts)*
Round 4: [2sc, 2sc in next st] 6 times. *(24 sts)*
Round 5: [3sc, 2sc in next st] 6 times. *(30 sts)*
Rounds 6–11: 1sc in each st around.
Fasten off and sew in the ends (see page 120).

SMALL SPOTS
(make 4)
Using B, make a magic ring.
Round 1: 6sc in magic ring. *(6 sts)*
Fasten off leaving a long tail to sew to cap.

LARGE SPOTS
(make 2)
Using B, make a magic ring.
Round 1: 6sc in magic ring. *(6 sts)*
Round 2: [2sc in next st] 6 times. *(12 sts)*
Fasten off leaving a long tail to sew to cap.

HANGING LOOP
Using A, ch11.
Row 1: Slst in second ch from hook, 9slst. *(10 sts)*
Fasten off leaving a long tail to sew to top
of cap.

HOUSE
Using C, ch13.
Round 1: 3sc in second ch from hook, 10sc,
3sc in last ch, working along opp side of chain,
10sc, slst in first sc. *(26 sts)*
Rounds 2–14: 1sc in each st around.
Fasten off leaving a long tail to sew to inside
of cap.

DOOR
Using D, ch5.
Round 1: 1sc in second ch from hook, 2sc, 3sc
in last ch, working along opp side of chain, 3sc.
Fasten off leaving a long tail to sew to house.

FINISHING
Sew spots onto cap. Thread a split ring onto
loop, bring ends of loop together and sew to
top of cap.
Using A, stitch a French knot (see page 126)
for door handle.
Using E, stitch 2 simple windows above door,
measuring 3 sts wide by 3 rows high.
Sew in all ends.

strawberry water bottle cover

Brighten up your day with this fun and colorful cover for your water bottle. The pattern features 3D stitches, a sewn-on strawberry motif, and a simple crocheted drawstring cord to keep your bottle safe.

SKILL RATING ● ● ●

YARN AND MATERIALS
Knitcraft Cotton Blend DK (50% cotton, 50% acrylic) light worsted (DK) weight yarn, 235yd (215m) per 3½oz (100g) ball

1 ball in each of:
Yellow 1008 (A)
Hot Pink 1003 (B)
Teal 1002 (C)
Bright Blue 1005 (D)

Large wooden bead

HOOK AND EQUIPMENT
US size G/6 (4mm) crochet hook

Yarn needle

FINISHED MEASUREMENTS
9½in (24cm) by 10¼in (26cm) circumference

ABBREVIATIONS
See page 126.

MAIN COVER
Using A, make a magic ring.
Round 1: 6sc into ring. *(6 sc)*
Round 2: [2sc in next st] 6 times. *(12 sc)*
Round 3: [1sc, 2sc in next st] 6 times. *(18 sc)*
Round 4: [2sc, 2sc in next st] 6 times. *(24 sc)*
Round 5: [3sc, 2sc in next st] 6 times. *(30 sc)*
Round 6: [4sc, 2sc in next st] 6 times. *(36 sc)*
Round 7: [5sc, 2sc in next st] 6 times. *(42 sc)*
Round 8: 1scBLO in each st around.
Rounds 9–12: 1sc in each st around.
Line of strawberries
Join B and carry across round, do not fasten off A.
Round 13: [2sc in A, 5dc in B in next st] 14 times.
Fasten off B.
Join C and carry across round, do not fasten off A.
Round 14: [2sc in A, dc5tog in C] 14 times.
Fasten off C, cont in A.
Rounds 15–19: 1sc into each st around. *(42 sc)*
Fasten off A, join D.
Middle band
Rounds 20–31: Rep Round 15.
Fasten off D, join A.
Rounds 32–36: Rep Round 15.
Line of strawberries
Rounds 37 and 38: Rep Rounds 13 and 14.
Fasten off B and C, do not fasten off A.
Rounds 39–43: Rep Round 15.
Round 44: [3sc, ch2, miss 2 sts] 8 times, 2sc. *(42 sts)*
Round 45: [3sc, 2sc in 2-ch sp] 8 times, 2sc. *(42 sc)*
Round 46: 1sc in each st around.
Round 47: [1sc, 2sc in next st] 21 times. *(63 sc)*
Rounds 48 and 49: 1sc in each st around.
Fasten off and sew in ends (see page 120).

CORD
Using D, ch100.
Row 1: 1slst in second ch from hook, 1slst in each ch to end. *(99 slst)*
Fasten off and sew in ends.

STRAWBERRY
Using B, make a magic ring.
Round 1: Ch3 (counts as 1dc), 12dc in ring, slst in top of beg 3-ch to join. *(13 dc)*
Round 2: Slst, (1hdc, 1dc) in next st, [3tr in next st] twice, [3dc in next st] twice, (2dc, 1tr) in next st, ch1, (1tr, 2dc) in next st, [3dc in next st] twice, [3tr in next st] twice, (1dc, 1hdc) in next st, slst in first slst to join. *(34 sts, one 1-ch sp)*
Fasten off leaving a long tail to sew to cover.

STALK
Round 1: Using C, [ch4, 1sc in second ch from hook, 2sc] 3 times, slst in first st to join.
Fasten off leaving a long tail to sew to strawberry.

FINISHING
Sew the strawberry to the middle band using the photograph as a guide. Sew the stalk to the top of the strawberry.
Thread the cord through the eyelet holes around the top of the cover, bringing both ends out of one eyelet. Thread both ends through the wooden bead, then knot each end.

With a pouch that doubles up as a game board, this little tic-tac-toe set is perfect for travel. For this two-player game, each person has five matching pieces and takes turns placing a piece in one of the squares. The first person to get three in a row horizontally, vertically, or diagonally is the winner! You could also make the bag on its own and use it for storing cosmetics or travel essentials.

sunshine and snails tic-tac-toe

YARN AND MATERIALS
Rico Ricorumi DK (100% cotton) light worsted (DK) weight yarn, 64yd (58m) per 1oz (25g) ball
1 ball in each of:
Rose 008 (A)
Red 028 (B)
Blue 032 (C)
Tangerine 026 (D)
Berry 015 (E)
Pistachio 047 (F)
Pastel Yellow 062 (G)
2 wooden beads, 1in (25mm)
Small piece of felt in each of two colors

HOOK AND EQUIPMENT
US size E/4 (3.5mm) crochet hook

Yarn needle

Pencil

Fabric scissors

FINISHED MEASUREMENTS
Bag: 9½in (24cm) square
Snail: 3in (7cm) wide x 2in (5cm) high
Sunshine: 2¾in (6.5cm) diameter

ABBREVIATIONS
See page 126.

BAG
Do not carry yarns across. Use a separate ball of yarn for each section.
Using A, ch15, using B, ch15, using A, ch16.
Row 1 (RS): 1sc in second ch from hook using A, 14sc using A, 15sc using B, 15sc using A, turn. *(45 sc)*
Rows 2–14: Ch1, 15sc using A, 15sc using B, 15sc using A, turn.
Fasten off all yarns. Join again as needed.
Rows 15–28: Ch1, 15sc using B, 15sc using A, 15sc using B, turn.
Fasten off all yarns. Join again as needed.
Rows 29–42: Ch1, 15sc using A, 15sc using B, 15sc using A, turn.
Fasten off all yarns, join D.
Rows 43–84: Ch1, 1sc in each st, turn.
Fasten off D and sew in ends (see page 120).
Define squares by working surface crochet/chain stitch (see page 123) along edges using C.

Fold panel in half, join C to top corner. Work 1sc in each row end, through both pieces to join sides of bag together (see page 122).
Rep on other side.
Fasten off and sew in the ends.

Top edging
Join C to top RH side of bag.
Work in continuous rounds.
Rounds 1–4: 1sc in each st. (90 sc)
Round 5 (drawstring holes): [2sc, miss 2 sts, ch2] 22 times, 2sc.
Round 6: [2sc, 2sc in 2ch-sp] 22 times, 2sc. *(90 sc)*
Rounds 7–9: 1sc in each st. *(90 sc)*
Fasten off and sew in ends.

DRAWSTRING
Using D, ch120.
Row 1: 1slst in second ch from hook, 1slst in each ch. *(119 slst)*
Fasten off and sew in ends.

NAIL

(make 5)

Using E, make a magic ring.

Round 1: 6sc in ring. *(6 sc)*

Round 2: [2sc in same st] 6 times. *(12 sc)*

Round 3: [1sc, 2sc in next st] 6 times. *(18 sc)*

Round 4: [2sc, 2sc in next st] 6 times. *(24 sc)*

Fasten off E, join F.

Row 5: 9sc, turn.

Row 6: Ch1, (does not count as st), 3sc in first st, 8sc, [hdc, 2hdc) in next st of snail shell (Round 4), miss next [st] of Round 4, 1sc, turn. *(18 sts)*

Row 7: Ch3, slst in second ch, slst in next ch, slst in sc, [ch]3, slst in second ch, 1sc in first of the 4dc from prev [row], 2hdc in next dc, (1hdc, 1sc) in next dc, slst in next [st], slst in each rem st to end.

Fasten off and sew in ends.

SUNSHINE

(make 5)

Using G, make a magic ring.

Round 1: 6sc in ring. *(6 sc)*

Round 2: [2sc in same st] 6 times. *(12 sc)*

Round 3: [1sc, 2sc in next st] 6 times. *(18 sc)*

Round 4: [2sc, 2sc in next st] 6 times. *(24 sc)*

Round 5: [3sc, 2sc in next st] 6 times. *(36 sc)*

Fasten off G, join D.

Round 6: (1sc, ch3, 1sc) in first st, slst in next st, *(1sc, ch3, 1sc) in next st, slst in next st; rep from * 16 times.

Fasten off and sew in ends.

FINISHING

Thread drawstring in and out through holes in Round 5 of bag. Thread a 1in (25mm) wooden bead onto each end of cord and tie a knot below to secure. Using a contrasting color felt, draw around each motif and cut out. Use fabric glue to stick to back of each motif.

CHAPTER 3
Beautiful Wreaths
& Decorations

bee and flower mobile

Add a playful touch to any room with this colorful and unique decoration. You could personalize your mobile by adding crocheted pieces from different projects, such as the heart from page 108 or mushrooms from page 110.

See page 108 or mushrooms from page 110.

SKILL RATING ● ● ○

YARN AND MATERIALS
Rico Ricorumi DK (100% cotton) light worsted (DK) weight yarn, 64yd (58m) per 1oz (25g) ball
1 ball in each of:
White 001 (A)
Green 049 (B)
Yellow 006 (C)
Fuchsia 014 (D)
Sky Blue 031 (E)
Chocolate 057 (F)

6in (15cm) embroidery hoop

9in (23cm) embroidery hoop

11 natural wooden beads,
1in (25mm) diameter

Small amount of fiber filling

Fabric glue if required

HOOK AND EQUIPMENT
US size C/2-D/3 (3mm) crochet hook
Yarn needle

FINISHED MEASUREMENTS
Bee: 4in (10cm) long
Daisy: 3in (7.5cm) diameter
Rainbow: 3½in (9cm) wide x 3½in (9cm) tall

ABBREVIATIONS
See page 126.

SPECIAL ABBREVIATION
Picot: Ch3, sl st in second ch from hook, sl st in next ch.

CLOUDS
Using A, ch81.
Round 1: 1sc in second ch from hook, 79sc to end. *(80 sc)*
Round 2: [Slst, miss 2 sts, 8tr in next st, miss 2 sts, slst, miss 1 st, 6dc in next st, miss 1 st] 8 times.
Fasten off and sew in ends (see page 120).

VINE
Using B, ch94.
Round 1: Slst in second ch from hook, [4slst in main ch, ch6, slst in second ch from hook, 4slst] 23 times, working along opp side of foundation ch, [ch6, slst in second ch from hook, 4slst, 4slst in main ch] 23 times.
Fasten off and sew in ends.

BEE
BEE BODY
(make 1 each in C, D, E)
Using first color, make a magic ring.
Round 1: 6sc in magic ring. *(6 sc)*
Round 2: [2sc in next st] 6 times. *(12 sc)*
Round 3: [1sc, 2sc in next st] 6 times. *(18 sc)*
Round 4: [2sc, 2sc in next st] 6 times. *(24 sc)*
Rounds 5-10: 1sc in each st.
Round 11: [2sc, sc2tog] 6 times. *(18 sc)*
Round 12: [1sc, sc2tog] 6 times. *(12 sc)*
Start to stuff with fiber filling.
Round 13: [Sc2tog] 6 times. *(6 sc)*
Change to F, do not fasten off first color.
Round 14: Working in FLO, [2sc in next st] 6 times. *(12 sc)*
Round 15: [1sc, 2sc in next st] 6 times. *(18 sc)*
Round 16: [2sc, 2sc in next st] 6 times. *(24 sc)*
Change to first color, do not fasten off F.

Rounds 17–19: 1sc in each st.
Change to F, do not fasten off first color.
Rounds 20–22: 1sc in each st.
Change to first color, fasten off F.
Round 23: [2sc, sc2tog] 6 times. *(18 sc)*
Round 24: [1sc, sc2tog] 6 times. *(12 sc)*
Continue to stuff with fiber filling.
Round 25: [Sc2tog] 6 times. *(6 sc)*
Fasten off, sew closed, sew in ends.

WING
(make 2 for each bee)
Using A, make a magic ring.
Round 1: 6sc in magic ring. *(6 sc)*
Round 2: [2sc in next st] 6 times. *(12 sc)*
Rounds 3–6: 1sc in each st.
Round 7: [2sc, sc2tog] 3 times. *(9 sc)*
Round 8: [1sc, sc2tog] 3 times. *(6 sc)*
Fasten off, sew closed, leaving long tail to sew
to body of bee.

ANTENNAE
(make 1 for each bee)
Using F, ch12.
Fasten off.
Using needle, pull ch through top of bee's head
to two equal lengths, forming two antennae.

DAISY
(make 6)
Using C, make a magic ring.
Round 1: 6sc in magic ring. *(6 sc)*
Round 2: [2sc in next st] 6 times. *(12 sc)*
Round 3: [1sc, 2sc in next st] 6 times. *(18 sc)*
Round 4: [2sc, 2sc in next st] 6 times. *(24 sc)*
Petals
Fasten off C, join A to any st.
Round 5: *(1sc, ch1, 1dc, 1tr) in next sc, (1tr, 1dc, ch1, 1sc)
in next sc, 1sc; rep from * 7 more times.
Fasten off leaving long end for sewing flowers tog.

LEAVES

(make 6)

Using B, ch9.

Round 1: 1sc in second ch from hook, 1hdc, 2dc, 3tr in next ch, 2dc, (2dc, picot, 2dc) in last ch, working along opp side of ch, 2dc, 3tr in next ch, 2dc, 1hdc, 1sc, slst in first sc, ch4, slst in second ch from hook, 2slst. Fasten off leaving long end for sewing leaves tog.

RAINBOW

(make 2)

Using E, ch16.

Row 1: 1sc in second ch from hook, 5sc, [2sc in next st] 3 times, 6sc, ch1, turn. *(18 sc)*

Row 2: 6sc, [1sc, 2sc in next st] 3 times, 6sc, ch1, turn. *(21 sc)*

Fasten off E, join B.

Row 3: 6sc, [2sc, 2sc in next st] 3 times, 6sc, ch1, turn. *(24 sc)*

Row 4: 6sc, [3sc, 2sc in next st] 3 times, 6sc, ch1, turn. *(27 sc)*

Fasten off B, join C.

Row 5: 6sc, [4sc, 2sc in next st] 3 times, 6sc, ch1, turn. *(30 sc)*

Row 6: 6sc, [5sc, 2sc in next st] 3 times, 6sc, ch1, turn. *(33 sc)*

Fasten off C, join D.

Row 7: 6sc, [6sc, 2sc in next st] 3 times, 6sc, ch1, turn. *(36 sc)*

Row 8: 6sc, [7sc, 2sc in next st] 3 times, 6sc, turn. *(39 sc)*

Fasten off leaving long end to sew rainbows tog.

FINISHING

Glue clouds around 9in (15cm) embroidery hoop. Glue vine around 6in (23cm) embroidery hoop. Sew or glue two flowers WS tog so you have three flowers in total. Sew or glue two leaves WS tog so you have three leaves in total. Sew two rainbows WS tog using D, so you have one rainbow. Cut four 40in (100cm) lengths of A. Knot all four lengths tog at top with first bead.

Middle hanging length

Thread and glue one bead 3in (8cm) from first bead. Thread on rainbow, 8in (20cm) from second bead. Evenly space and glue three more beads below rainbow. Middle hanging length should measure 18in (45cm), cut excess off.

Three side lengths

Must be identical or mobile may not hang evenly. Thread and glue one bead 3in (8cm) from first bead on all three lengths. Leave gap of 3in (8cm) then attach cloud hoop. Leave another gap of 2¾in (7cm) before attaching leaves. Attach vines hoop 2¾in (7cm) below leaves. Leave 4in (10cm) and attach bees, another 4in (10cm) gap and glue final beads. Lastly attach flowers after another 4in (10cm) gap.

With its beautiful fall colors, this versatile decoration would look gorgeous hanging on a door or displayed on a mantelpiece. This pattern uses loop stitch to create the grass and is a great way of practicing this technique.

mushroom wall décor

YARN AND MATERIALS
Rico Ricorumi DK (100% cotton) light worsted (DK) weight yarn, 64yd (58m) per 1oz (25g) ball
  1 ball in each of:
  Fox 025 (A)
  White 001 (B)
  Smokey Rose 010 (C)
  Mustard 064 (D)
  Pea 077 (E)
  Sky Blue 031 (F)
10in (25cm) diameter embroidery hoop

HOOK AND EQUIPMENT
US size C/2-D/3 (3mm) crochet hook
Yarn needle

FINISHED MEASUREMENTS
Small mushroom: 3in (7cm) tall
Medium mushroom: 4in (10cm) tall
Large mushroom: 4¾in (12.5cm) tall

ABBREVIATIONS
See page 126.

SPECIAL ABBREVIATION
Loop st (loop stitch): With the yarn over left index finger, insert the hook into the next st and draw two strands through the st (take the first strand from under the index finger and at the same time take the second strand from over the index finger). Pull the yarn to tighten loop, forming a 1½-in (4-cm) loop on index finger. Remove your finger from the loop, put the loop to the back of the work, yoh and pull through 3 loops on the hook (1 loop stitch made on right side of work).

SMALL MUSHROOM
CAP
Using A, make a magic ring.
Round 1: 6sc in magic ring. *(6 sc)*
Round 2: [2sc in next st] 6 times. *(12 sc)*
Round 3: 1sc in each st around.
Round 4: [1sc, 2sc in next st] 6 times. *(18 sc)*
Round 5: 1sc in each st around.
Round 6: [2sc, 2sc in next st] 6 times. *(24 sc)*
Round 7: 1sc in each st around.
Round 8: [3sc, 2sc in next st] 6 times. *(30 sc)*
Rounds 9 and 10: 1sc in each st around.
Fasten off and sew in ends (see page 120).

STALK
Using B, make a magic ring.
Round 1: 6sc in magic ring. *(6 sc)*
Round 2: [2sc in next st] 6 times. *(12 sc)*
Round 3: 1scBLO in each st around
Rounds 4–15: 1sc in each st around.
Round 16: [Sc2tog] 6 times. *(6 sc)*
Fasten off and sew closed, leaving long tail to sew to cap.

MEDIUM MUSHROOM

CAP
Using C, make a magic ring.
Rounds 1–8: Rep Rounds 1–8 of small mushroom. *(30 sc)*
Round 9: 1sc in each st around.
Round 10: [4sc, 2sc in next st] 6 times. *(36 sc)*
Rounds 11 and 12: 1sc in each st around.
Fasten off and sew in ends.

STALK
Using B, make a magic ring.
Round 1: 6sc in magic ring. *(6 sc)*
Round 2: [2sc in next st] 6 times. *(12 sc)*
Round 3: [1sc, 2sc in next st] 6 times. *(18 sc)*
Round 4: 1scBLO in each st around.
Rounds 5–18: 1sc in each st around.
Round 19: [1sc, sc2tog] 6 times. *(12 sc)*
Round 20: [Sc2tog] 6 times. *(6 sc)*
Fasten off and sew closed, leaving long tail to sew to cap.

LARGE MUSHROOM

CAP
Using D, make a magic ring.
Rounds 1–8: Rep Rounds 1–8 of small mushroom. *(30 sc)*
Round 9: 1sc in each st around.
Round 10: [4sc, 2sc in next st] 6 times. *(36 sc)*
Round 11: 1sc in each st around.
Round 12: [5sc, 2sc in next st] 6 times. *(42 sc)*
Rounds 13 and 14: 1sc in each st around.
Fasten off and sew in ends.

STALK
Using B, make a magic ring.
Round 1: 6sc in magic ring. *(6 sc)*
Round 2: [2sc in next st] 6 times. *(12 sc)*
Round 3: [1sc, 2sc in next st] 6 times. *(18 sc)*
Round 4: [2sc, 2sc in next st] 6 times. *(24 sc)*
Round 5: 1scBLO in each st around.
Rounds 6–21: 1sc in each st around.
Round 22: [2sc, sc2tog] 6 times. *(18 sc)*
Round 23: [1sc, sc2tog] 6 times. *(12 sc)*
Round 24: [Sc2tog] 6 times. *(6 sc)*

Fasten off and sew closed, leaving long tail to sew to cap.

SMALL SPOTS
(make 4 in each of D, C, A)
Make a magic ring.
Round 1: 6sc in magic ring. *(6 sc)*
Fasten off.

BIG SPOTS
(make 1 in A, 2 in C)
Make a magic ring.
Round 1: 6sc in magic ring. *(6 sc)*
Round 2: [2sc in next st] 6 times. *(12 sc)*
Fasten off.

GRASS
Using E, ch41.
Row 1: 1sc in second ch from hook, 1sc in each ch to end, ch1, turn. *(40 sc)*
Row 2: Work loop st in each st, ch1, turn *(40 loop sts)*
Row 3: 1sc in each st, ch1, turn.
Rows 4-7: Rep Rows 2 and 3 twice more.
Row 8: Work loop st (see page 125) in each st.
Fasten off leaving long tail to sew around bottom of embroidery hoop.

BOW
Using F, ch61.
Row 1: Slst in second ch from hook, 59 slst. *(60 slst)*
Fasten off and sew in ends.

FINISHING
Sew grass around bottom part of embroidery hoop.
Sew 4 small spots in D to small cap, then sew cap to stalk.
Sew 4 small spots, 1 large spot in A to medium cap, then sew cap to stalk.
Sew 4 small spots, 2 large spots in C to large cap, then sew cap to stalk.
Sew mushrooms in size order along grass.
Tie bow around top of hoop.

Decorate your home with beautiful spring flowers all year round with this pot of crocheted blooms. Yarn is wrapped around pieces of wire to create the stems, and crocheted soil is added to the pot. Several of these flowers tied together with ribbon would make a lovely birthday gift.

lovely flower pot

YARN AND MATERIALS
Rico Ricorumi DK (100% cotton) light worsted (DK) weight yarn, 64yd (58m) per 1oz (25g) ball
1 ball in each of:
Orchid 016 (A)
Pastel Yellow 062 (B)
White 001 (C)
Green 049 (D)
Candy Pink 012 (E)
Red 028 (F)
Berry 015 (G)
Pistachio 047 (H)
Pea 077 (I)
Chocolate 057 (J)
8 lengths of wire, each 13¾in (35cm) long
Fiber filling
Terracotta plant pot

HOOK AND EQUIPMENT
3.5mm (US size E/4) crochet hook
Yarn needle
Glue gun

FINISHED MEASUREMENTS
Lavender: 13in (33cm)
Daisy: 10½in (27cm)
Tulip: 11½in (29cm)
Leafy sprig: 13½in (34cm)

ABBREVIATIONS
See page 126.

LAVENDER
(make 2)
Using A, ch100.
Starting in second ch from hook, (slst, 3ch, slst) in each st to end.
Fasten off and sew in ends (see page 120).

DAISY
(make 2)
Using B, make a magic ring.
Round 1: 6sc in magic ring. *(6 sc)*
Round 2: [2sc in next st] 6 times. *(12 sc)*
Round 3: [1sc, 2sc in next st] 6 times. *(18 sc)*
Round 4: [2sc, 2sc in next st] 6 times. *(24 sc)*
Petals
Fasten off B, join C.
Round 5: *slst, (slst, ch3, 1tr) in next st, (1tr, ch3, slst) in next st; rep from * 7 more times.
Fasten off and sew in ends.

DAISY LEAF
(make 4)
Using D, ch6.
Row 1: 1sc in second ch from hook, 1hdc, 2dc in next ch, 1dc, 4dc in last ch, working along opp side of chain, 1dc, 2dc in next ch, 1hdc, 1sc, slst in first sc.
Fasten off leaving a long tail to attach to stem.

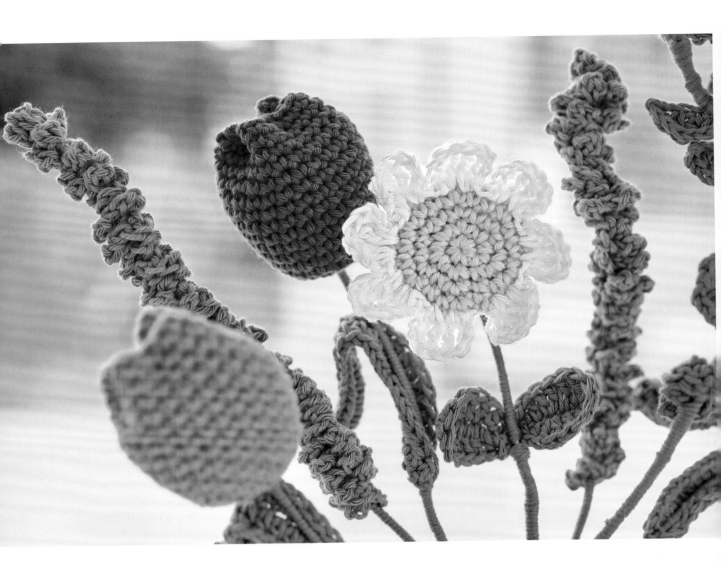

TULIP

(make 1 in each of E, F, G)
Make a magic ring.
Round 1: 6sc in magic ring. *(6 sc)*
Round 2: [2sc in next st] 6 times. *(12 sc)*
Round 3: [1sc, 2sc in next st] 6 times. *(18 sc)*
Round 4: [2sc, 2sc in next st] 6 times. *(24 sc)*
Rounds 5–16: 1sc in each st.
Fasten off leaving a long tail to sew closed.

TULIP LEAF

(make 3)
Using H, ch24.
Round 1: 1sc in second ch from hook, 1hdc, 20dc, 4dc in last ch, working along opp side of chain, 20dc, 1hdc, 1sc.
Fasten off and sew in ends.

LEAFY SPRIG

(make 13)
Using I, ch6.
Row 1: 1sc in the second ch from hook, 1hdc, 1dc, 1hdc, (1sc, slst) in last ch.
Fasten off leaving a long tail to attach to stem.

SOIL

Using J, ch6, join with slst to make a ring.
Round 1: 12sc in ring (this creates center hole for flower stems). *(12 sts)*
Round 2: [1sc, 2sc in next st] 6 times. *(18 sts)*
Round 3: [2sc, 2sc in next st] 6 times. *(24 sts)*
Round 4: [3sc, 2sc in next st] 6 times. *(30 sts)*
Round 5: [4sc, 2sc in next st] 6 times. *(36 sts)*
Round 6: [5sc, 2sc in next st] 6 times. *(42 sts)*
Round 7: [6sc, 2sc in next st] 6 times. *(48 sts)*
Round 8: [7sc, 2sc in next st] 6 times. *(54 sts)*

ound 9: [8sc, 2sc in next st] 6 times. *(60 sts)*
ound 10: 1sc in each st around.

INISHING

sing a glue gun, wrap each lavender strip around a
•ngth of wire, gluing as you go. It should cover about
•ne third of length. Using D, wrap around rest of wire,
luing in place as you go.

asten each daisy head to top of a wire and glue in
•lace. Wrap wire with D, wrapping along whole length
•f and adding two leaves to each stem, hiding yarn
•nds as you go.

•sert a length of wire in each tulip head, bend over top
•f wire and glue in place inside tulip head. Lightly stuff
•ith fiber filling. Press two sides of the top together
•nd sew in place. Now press other two sides together
•nd sew in place, to form a cross shape for top of tulip.
•sing H, wrap around the rest of the length of wire
•elow the tulip heads, adding one leaf and gluing in
•ace as you go.

Add leafy sprigs around top third of remaining wire
and cont to wrap using I down stem.
Use some fiber filling to stuff terracotta pot.
Thread all finished flowers through center hole in soil
and glue stem ends before pushing inside pot. Glue
soil to inside rim of pot.

SKILL RATING ● ● ●

YARN AND MATERIALS
Rico Ricorumi DK (100% cotton)
light worsted (DK) weight yarn,
64yd (58m) per 1oz (25g) ball
  1 ball in each of:
  Fuchsia 014 (A)
  Yellow 006 (B)
  Sky Blue 031 (C)
12in (30cm) diameter circular mirror

HOOK AND EQUIPMENT
US size E/4 (3.5mm) crochet hook
Yarn needle
Glue gun

FINISHED MEASUREMENTS
Each flower: 2¼in (5.5cm) across

ABBREVIATIONS
See page 126.

COLORWAYS
Fuchsia with Yellow center
Sky Blue with Fuchsia center
Yellow with Sky Blue center

daisy chain mirror

Add a splash of color to a plain mirror with this simple design.
The flowers are quick to make, and you can get creative by
mixing and matching your colors for each one. The finished
design would make a beautiful centerpiece for any room.

FLOWERS
(make 4 of each colorway)
Using center color, make a magic ring.
Round 1: Ch3 (counts as first dc), 1dc, ch1, *2dc, ch1; rep
from * 4 more times.
Fasten off center color, join petal color in ch sp from Round
1 and work in each ch sp around.
Round 2: [Slst into ch sp, ch3] 6 times, slst into first slst
to join.
Round 3: Working in 3 ch sps from Round 2, [slst, ch2,
3dc, ch2, slst] in each ch-sp to create 6 petals.
Fasten off and sew in ends (see page 120).

FINISHING
Glue all flowers around mirror using glue gun.

Bring the outdoors inside with this pretty garland embellished with 3D roses. Hooked up in beautiful bulky yarn, this garland would look lovely strung from the ceiling, hung on a door, or draped across a table.

roses garland

SKILL RATING ● ● ○

YARN AND MATERIALS
Knitcraft Return Of Mac Yarn
(100% cotton) bulky (chunky)
weight yarn, 88½yd (81m)
per 7oz (200g) ball
1 ball of Sage 1007 (A)

Knitcraft Join the Dots (80%
acrylic, 20% wool) bulky (chunky)
weight yarn, 208yd (190m) per
3½oz (100g) ball
1 ball in each of:
 Cream Print 1002 (B)
 Purple Print 1000 (C)
 Blue Print 1003 (D)

HOOK AND EQUIPMENT
US size J/10 (6mm) crochet hook
Yarn needle

FINISHED MEASUREMENTS
Flower: 3½in (9cm) across
Leaf: 4¼in (11cm) long
Garland: 47¼in (120cm) long

ABBREVIATIONS
See page 126.

SPECIAL ABBREVIATION
Picot: Ch3, slst in second ch
from hook, slst in next ch.

GARLAND
Using A, ch122.
Row 1: 1hdc in third ch from hook, 1hdc in each ch to end. *(120 hdc)*
Fasten off and sew in ends (see page 120).

LEAVES
(make 14)
Using B, ch9.
Round 1: 1dc in fifth ch from hook (missed 4 ch counts as 1 dc and one foundation ch), 3dc, (2dc 1tr, picot, 1tr, 2dc) in last ch, working along opp side of chain, 4dc, 4dc in beg foundation ch, sl st to in third ch of beg dc to join.
Fasten off and sew in ends.

ROSE
(make 4 in C, 3 in D)
Ch25.
Row 1: 1dc in fifth ch from hook (missed 4 ch counts as 1dc, ch2), *miss next ch, (1dc, ch2, 1dc) in next ch; rep from * 9 times, turn. *(11 v-sts)*
Row 2: Ch1, 6dc in first 2-ch sp, *1sc between next 2 dc, 6dc in next 2-ch sp; rep from * to end. *(11 petals)*
Fasten off leaving a long tail.

FINISHING
Roll rose from one end and stitch in place.
Using photo as a guide, sew pair of leaves and alternate color rose spaced at intervals along garland.
Sew in ends.

Go bright and colorful with this fantastic floral bunting. The pattern uses granny stitches to create the triangle shapes, and the pieces are crocheted together along the top so no sewing up is required!

daisy chain bunting

BUNTING TRIANGLES
(make 6)
Using A, make a magic ring.
Round 1: Ch3 (counts as 1dc), 11dc in ring. *(12 dc (6 x 2-dc sets))*
Fasten off A, join B between 2-dc sets from Round 1.
Round 2: [1sc between 2-dc sets, ch3] 6 times, slst in first sc to join.
Round 3: Working in 3-ch sps from Round 2, *(slst, ch3, 3tr, ch3, slst) in 3-ch sp, ch1; rep from * 5 times, slst around first 3-ch to join. *(6 petals)*
Fasten off B, join C in 1-ch sp from Round 3.
Round 4: (Slst, ch3) in each 1-ch sp from Round 3, slst around first ch-3 to join.

SKILL RATING ● ● ○

YARN AND MATERIALS
Women's Institute Premium Acrylic Yarn (100% acrylic) light worsted (DK) weight yarn, 273yd (250m) per 3½oz (100g) ball
   1 ball in each of:
   Yellow 1025 (A)
   White 1000 (B)
   Green 1001 (C)
   Soft Pink 1026 (D)
   Soft Blue 1025 (E)

HOOK AND EQUIPMENT
US size G/6 (4mm) crochet hook
Yarn needle

FINISHED MEASUREMENTS
Triangle: 7in (18cm) wide by 6¼in (16cm) tall
Bunting: 73in (186cm) long

ABBREVIATIONS
See page 126.

Round 5: (Ch4 (counts as 1tr), 2tr, ch2, 3tr) in first 3-ch [s]p (corner), ch2, 3hdc in next 3-ch sp, *(3tr, ch2, 3tr) in [n]ext 3-ch sp, ch2, 3hdc in next 3-ch sp; rep from * once [m]ore, slst in fourth ch of beg ch-4 to join.

Round 6: Ch4 (counts as 1dc, ch1), *(3dc, ch2, 3dc) in [fi]rst 2-ch sp (corner), ch1, 3dc in next 2-ch sp, ch1, 3dc in [n]ext 2-ch sp, ch1; rep from * once more, (3dc, ch2, 3dc) [i]n next 2-ch sp, ch1, 3dc in next 2-ch sp, ch1, 2dc in next [-]ch sp, slst in third ch of beg 4-ch to join.
[F]asten off C, join D in any 2-ch corner sp.

Round 7: Ch2 (counts as first hdc in foll instructions), [w]ork (3hdc, ch2, 3hdc) in each corner sp, 1hdc in top [o]f each dc from Round 6 and 1dc in each 1-ch sp, all [a]round, slst in first st to join. *(63 sts, three 2-ch sp)*

Round 8: Ch1 (does not count as a st), 1sc in each st [a]round and (2sc, ch1, 2sc) in each corner sp to end, [sl]st in first st to join. *(75 sts, three 1-ch sp)*
[F]asten off D, join E in any corner 1-ch sp.

Round 9: Ch 1 (does not count as a st), 1sc in 1-ch sp, [m]iss next st, *(ch3, 1sc) in next st, miss next st/sp; [r]ep from * along two sides of triangle, ending with [1]sc in last 1-ch sp.

Fasten off and sew in ends (see page 120).

FINISHING
Using E, ch40.
Row 1: *1sc in each sc in top (last side) of triangle, ch5; rep from * to join each triangle, ch40, turn.
Row 2: Starting in second ch, 1sc in each ch and st to end, ch1, turn.
Row 3: *1sc, ch3, miss next st; rep from * to end, ending with 1sc in last st.
Fasten off and sew in the ends.

YARN AND MATERIALS
Rico Ricorumi DK (100% cotton) light worsted (DK) weight yarn, 64yd (58m) per 1oz (25g) ball
   1 ball in each of:
   Red 028 (A)
   Yellow 006 (B)
   Green 049 (C)
   Sky Blue 031 (D)
   Orchid 016 (E)
   Candy Pink 012 (F)
   Lilac 017 (G)

HOOK AND EQUIPMENT
US size E/4 (3.5mm) crochet hook

Yarn needle

FINISHED MEASUREMENTS
Approx 30in (76cm) long

ABBREVIATIONS
See page 126.

Update your décor with this quick and simple paper-chain-style decoration. This is a great stashbuster project, and you could add a new link whenever you have spare yarn to use up. Crochet one of these in holiday shades to make a festive version that you can bring out every year.

frilly crochet chain

CHAIN LINK
(make 3 in each of colors A, B, C, D, E, and F)
For each chain link, crochet through prev chain link to attach tog. Make all links in same way, changing colors for each.
Ch20, slst in first ch to form a ring.
Rounds 1–3: Ch1 (does not count as st), 1hdc in each st around, slst in first st to join. *(20 hdc)*
Fasten off.
Frill first side
Join G to any st.
Round 4: [1sc, miss 1 st, ch3] to end of round.
Fasten off.
Frill second side
Rep frill first side on other side of chain link.

FINISHING
Sew in ends (see page 120).

With sweet ladybugs, daisies, and a mini heart, this multicolored wreath would look wonderful hung up on a door or displayed on a shelf. You could even use the rainbow wreath as a base and decorate it with different embellishments such as the forget-me-nots and roses from pages 112–113.

rainbow wreath

SKILL RATING ● ● ●

YARN AND MATERIALS
Rico Ricorumi DK (100% cotton) light worsted (DK) weight yarn, 64yd (58m) per 1oz (25g) ball
1 ball in each of:
Purple 020 (A)
Lilac 017 (B)
Pink 011 (C)
Red 028 (D)
Smokey Orange 024 (E)
Tangerine 026 (F)
Yellow 006 (G)
Pastel Green 045 (H)
Turquoise 039 (I)
Light Blue 033 (J)
White 001 (K)
Grass Green 044 (L)
Black 060 (M)
Sky Blue 031 (N)

12in (30cm) polystyrene wreath base

2 pairs of safety eyes, ½in (8mm) diameter

Fiber filling

HOOK AND EQUIPMENT
US size E/4 (3.5mm) crochet hook
Yarn needle

FINISHED MEASUREMENTS
12in (30cm) diameter

ABBREVIATIONS
See page 126.

WREATH COVER
Work in a random rainbow color order using yarns A–J, varying number of rows in each color.
Ch36.
Row 1: 1sc in second ch from hook, 34sc, turn. *(35 sc)*
Rows 2–184: Ch1 (does not count as st throughout), 1sc in each st to end, turn.
Row 185: Ch1, 1sc in each st to end.
Fasten off leaving long tail to sew Row 1 to Row 185.

LARGE DAISY
(make 4)
Using G, make a magic ring.
Round 1: 6sc in ring. *(6 sc)*
Round 2: 2sc in each st. *(12 sc)*
Round 3: [1sc, 2sc in next st] 6 times. *(18 sc)*
Fasten off G, join K.
Round 4: *(Slst, ch4, 2tr) in first st, (2tr, ch4, slst) in next st, slst; rep from * 5 times.
Fasten off.

LARGE LEAVES
(make 4)
Using L, ch10.
Round 1: 1sc in second ch, 1sc, 1hdc, 1dc, 1tr, 1dc, 1hdc, 1sc, 3sc in last ch, working along opp side of chain, 1sc, 1hdc, 1dc, 1tr, 1dc, 1hdc, 1sc, 2sc in last ch, slst in first sc.
Round 2: Ch1, 1sc in same st, 1sc, 1hdc, 2dc in next st, 3dc in next st, 2dc in next st, 3hdc, (2hdc, ch2, 2hdc) in next st, 3hdc, 2dc in next st, 3dc in next st, 2dc in next st, 1hdc, 2sc, 3sc in next st, slst in first st.
Fasten off and sew in ends (see page 120).

HEART

Using D, make a magic ring.
Round 1: Ch3 (counts as a dc), 3tr, 3dc, ch1, 1tr, ch1, 3dc, 3tr, ch3, slst in ring.
Fasten off and sew in ends.

LADYBUG
HEAD AND BODY
(make 2)
Using M, make a magic ring.
Round 1: 6sc in ring. *(6 sc)*
Round 2: 2sc in each st. *(12 sc)*
Round 3: [1sc, 2sc in next st] 6 times. *(18 sc)*
Round 4: [2sc, 2sc in next st] 6 times. *(24 sc)*
Round 5: [3sc, 2sc in next st] 6 times. *(30 sc)*
Rounds 6–11: 1sc in each st.
Insert safety eyes between Rounds 8 and 9, 6 sts apart.
Sew a simple mouth between Rounds 9 and 10, 3 sts apart.
Round 12: [3sc, sc2tog] 6 times. *(24 sc)*
Start to stuff with fiber filling.
Round 13: [2sc, sc2tog] 6 times. *(18 sc)*
Round 14: [1sc, sc2tog] 6 times. *(12 sc)*
Round 15: [Sc2tog] 6 times. *(6 sc)*
Round 16: 2sc in each st. *(12 sc)*
Round 17: [1sc, 2sc in next st] 6 times. *(18 sc)*
Round 18: [2sc, 2sc in next st] 6 times. *(24 sc)*
Rounds 19–24: 1sc in each st.
Round 25: [2sc, sc2tog] 6 times. *(18 sc)*
Round 26: [1sc, sc2tog] 6 times. *(12 sc)*
Round 27: [Sc2tog] 6 times. *(6 sc)*
Fasten off and sew gap closed.

WING
(make 4)
Using D, make a magic ring.
Round 1: 6sc in ring. *(6 sc)*
Round 2: 2sc in each st. *(12 sc)*
Round 3: [1sc, 2sc in next st] 6 times. *(18 sc)*
Rounds 4–6: 1sc in each st.
Round 7: [1sc, sc2tog] 6 times. *(12 sc)*
Rounds 8–10: 1sc in each st.
Round 11: [2sc, sc2tog] 3 times. *(9 sc)*
Rounds 12–13: 1sc in each st.
Fasten off leaving a tail to sew to body.

SMALL DAISY

(make 3)
Using G, make a magic ring.
Round 1: 6sc in ring. *(6 sc)*
Round 2: 2sc in each st. *(12 sc)*
Fasten off G, join K.
Round 3: *(slst, ch3, 2dc, ch3, slst) in first st, slst; rep from * 5 times.
Fasten off.

SMALL LEAVES

(make 7)
Using L, ch9.
Round 1: 1sc in second ch from hook, 1hdc, 1dc, 2tr, 1dc, 1hdc, 3sc in last ch, working along opp side of chain, 1hdc, 1dc, 2tr, 1dc, 1hdc, 1sc, slst in first st.
Fasten off and sew in ends.

SPOT
(make 3 for each wing)

Using M, make a magic ring.

Round 1: 6sc in ring, slst in first st. *(6 sc)*

Fasten off leaving a tail to sew to wing.

ANTENNA
(make 2)

Using M, ch20

Row 1: Slst in second ch, 18 slst.

Fasten off leaving a tail to sew to head.

LEG
(make 4)

Using M, make a magic ring.

Round 1: 6sc in ring. *(6 sc)*

Round 2: 2sc in each st. *(12 sc)*

Rounds 3–4: 1sc in each st.

Round 5: [2sc, sc2tog] 3 times. *(9 sc)*

Round 6: [1sc, sc2tog] 3 times. *(6 sc)*

Rounds 7–10: 1sc in each st.

Lightly stuff with fiber filling.

Fasten off leaving a tail to sew to body.

ARM
(make 4)

Using M, make a magic ring.

Round 1: 6sc in ring. *(6 sc)*

Round 2: [1sc, 2sc in next st] 3 times. *(9 sc)*

Round 3: 1sc in each st.

Round 4: [1sc, sc2tog] 3 times. *(6 sc)*

Rounds 5–8: 1sc in each st.

Lightly stuff with fiber filling.

Fasten off leaving a tail to sew to body.

BOW TIE
(make 1)

Using N, make a magic ring.

Round 1: [Ch3, 3tr, ch3, slst] twice in ring.

Fasten off leaving a long tail.

FINISHING
Sew short ends of wreath cover together to make ring. Place wreath cover around polystyrene wreath. Sew sides together to encase wreath. Sew in ends.

Using photo as a guide, sew daisies and leaves around bottom half of wreath.

Sew spots to wings, arms to each side of body, legs to underside of body and wings to back of each ladybug. Thread an antenna through top of each ladybug head and sew in place. Wrap

tail of bowtie around middle four to six times, sew to secure, and sew onto ladybug. Position both ladybugs on wreath and sew in place. Attach heart to top center front of wreath.

gnome's washing wreath

Welcome guests to your home with this cute and quirky design.
Gorgeous flowers, mini toadstools, and a sun decorate the wreath
and the mini gnome and washing line add adorable finishing touches.

YARN AND MATERIALS
Rico Ricorumi DK (100% cotton) light
worsted (DK) weight yarn, 64yd (58m)
per 1oz (25g) ball
1 ball in each of:
Wine Red 029 (A)
Beige 055 (B)
Blue 032 (C)
Silver Gray 058 (D)
Black 060 (E)
White 001 (F)
Yellow 006 (G)
Lilac 017 (H)
Orange 027 (I)
Smokey Orange 024 (J)

Tangerine 026 (K)
Fuchsia 014 (L)
Pink 011 (M)
Green 049 (N)
Pistachio 047 (O)
Caramel 053 (P)
Pair of safety eyes ½in
(10mm) diameter
Fiber filling
String for washing line
6 miniature wooden pegs
Wicker wreath, 12in (30cm) diameter

HOOK AND EQUIPMENT
US size E/4 (3.5mm) crochet hook
Yarn needle

FINISHED MEASUREMENTS
Wreath: 30cm (12in) diameter

ABBREVIATIONS
See page 126.

SPECIAL ABBREVIATION
PC (popcorn): work 6dc all in one st,
remove live loop from hook, insert
hook in top of first dc, place loop
on hook and pull through.

GNOME
HAT
Using A, make a magic ring.
Round 1: 6sc in ring. (6 sc)
Round 2: 1sc in each st.
Round 3: [1sc, 2sc in next st] 3 times. (9 sc)
Round 4: 1sc in each st.
Round 5: [2sc, 2sc in next st] 3 times. (12 sc)
Round 6: 1sc in each st.
Round 7: [3sc, 2sc in next st] 3 times. (15 sc)
Round 8: 1sc in each st.
Round 9: [4sc, 2sc in next st] 3 times. (18 sc)
Fasten off leaving long tail to sew to head.

HEAD AND BODY
Using B, make a magic ring. Work in a continuous spiral.
Round 1: 6sc in ring. (6 sc)
Round 2: 2sc in each st. (12 sc)
Round 3: [1sc, 2sc in next st] 6 times. (18 sc)
Round 4: 1sc in each st.
Round 5: 9sc, PC, 8sc. (18 sts)
Round 6: Rep Round 4.
Insert safety eyes either side of nose.
Start to stuff with fiber filling.
Round 7: [1sc, sc2tog] 6 times. (12 sc)
Round 8: [Sc2tog] 6 times (6 sc)
Fasten off B, join C.
Round 9: 2sc in each st. (12 sc)
Round 10: [1sc, 2sc in next st] 6 times. (18 sc)
Rounds 11-13: 1sc in each st. (18 sc)
Fasten off C, join D.
Rounds 14 and 15: 1sc in each st.

Round 16: [1sc, sc2tog] 6 times. (12 sc)
Round 17: [Sc2tog] 6 times. (6 sc)
Fasten off and sew gap closed.

ARMS/LEGS
(make 2 in B/C for arms, 2 in E/D for legs)
Using B or E, make a magic ring.
Round 1: 6sc in ring. (6 sc)
Round 2: 1sc in each st.
Fasten off B or E, join C or D.
Rounds 3-8: 1sc in each st.
Do not stuff, fasten off leaving long tail to sew to body.

BEARD
Using F, make a magic ring.
Row 1: 3sc in ring, ch1, turn. (3 sc)
Row 2: 2sc in each st, ch1, turn. (6 sc)
Row 3: [1sc, 2sc in next st] 3 times. (9 sc)
Fasten off leaving long tail to sew beard to face.

GNOME'S WASHING
TROUSERS
Using P, make a magic ring.
Round 1: 6sc in ring. (6 sc)
Rounds 2-6: 1sc in each st.
Fasten off first leg.
Using P, make a magic ring.
Rep Rounds 1 to 6 for second leg, do not fasten off.
Cont working around first leg to join with second leg.
Rounds 7-10: 1sc in each st. (12 sc)
Fasten off and sew in ends (see page 120).

HAT
Using G, make a magic ring.
Round 1: 6sc in ring. *(6 sc)*
Round 2: 1sc in each st.
Round 3: [1sc, 2sc in next st] 3 times. *(9 sc)*
Round 4: 1sc in each st.
Round 5: [2sc, 2sc in next st] 3 times. *(12 sc)*
Round 6: 1sc in each st.
Round 7: [3sc, 2sc in next st] 3 times. *(15 sc)*
Rounds 8 and 9: 1sc in each st.
Fasten off and sew in ends.

JUMPER
Using A, ch10, slst in first ch to form a ring. *(10 sts)*
Round 1: Ch1 (does not count as a st throughout), *1sc, (1sc, ch1, 1sc), 2sc, (1sc, ch1, 1sc); rep from * once more, slst in first st. *(14 sc, 4 ch sps)*
Round 2: Ch1, 2sc, (1sc, ch1, 1sc) in ch sp, 4sc, (1sc, ch1, 1sc) in ch sp, 3sc, (1sc, ch1, 1sc) in ch sp, 4sc, (1sc, ch1, 1sc), 1sc, slst in first st. *(22 sc, 4 ch sps)*
Round 3: Ch1, 3sc, fold next two ch sps tog, insert hook through next 2 ch sps and work slst (missed sts will form sleeve), 5sc to next ch sp, insert hook through next 2 ch sps and work slst, 1sc in last 2 sts, slst in first st. *(10 sc)*
Round 4: Ch1, 2sc, [2sc in next st] twice, 3sc, [2sc in next st] twice, 1sc, slst in first st. *(14 sc)*
Rounds 5-7: Ch1, 14sc around, slst in first st.
Fasten off and sew in ends.
Sleeve
Join yarn to the underarm st of one set of missed sts from Round 3.
Round 1: Ch1, sc2tog, 2sc, sc2tog, slst in first st. *(4 sc)*
Rounds 2 and 3: Ch1, 4sc, slst in first st.
Fasten off.
Rep for second sleeve on other side.

FORGET-ME-NOT
(make 5 in C, 3 in H)
Using G, make a magic ring.
Round 1: Ch1 (does not count as st), 5sc in ring, slst in first sc. *(5 sc)*
Fasten off G, join C or H.
Round 2: (Ch2, 2dc, ch2, slst) in each st, slst in first st. *(5 petals)*
Fasten off and sew in ends.

LARGE MUSHROOM
CAP
Using I, make a magic ring.
Round 1: 6sc in ring. *(6 sc)*

Round 2: 2sc in each st. *(12 sc)*
Round 3: [1sc, 2sc in next st] 6 times. *(18 sc)*
Round 4: [2sc, 2sc in next st] 6 times. *(24 sc)*
Round 5: [3sc, 2sc in next st] 6 times *(30 sc)*
Rounds 6 and 7: 1sc in each st.
Fasten off and sew in ends.

STALK
Using F, make a magic ring.
Round 1: 6sc in ring. *(6 sc)*
Round 2: 2sc in each st. *(12 sc)*
Round 3: [1sc, 2sc in next st] 6 times. *(18 sc)*
Round 4: [2scBLO, 2scBLO in next st] 6 times. *(24 sc)*
Rounds 5-12: 1sc in each st.
Fasten off leaving long tail to sew to inside of cap, sew in ends.

MEDIUM MUSHROOM
CAP
Using J, make a magic ring.
Round 1: 6sc in ring. *(6 sc)*
Round 2: 2sc in each st. *(12 sc)*
Round 3: [1sc, 2sc in next st] 6 times. *(18 sc)*
Round 4: [2sc, 2sc in next st] 6 times. *(24 sc)*
Rounds 5 and 6: 1sc in each st.
Fasten off and sew in ends.

STALK
Using F, make a magic ring.
Round 1: 6sc in ring. *(6 sc)*
Round 2: 2sc in each st. *(12 sc)*
Round 3: [1scBLO, 2scBLO in next st] 6 times. *(18 sc)*
Rounds 4-9: 1sc in each st.
Fasten off leaving long tail to sew to inside of cap, sew in ends.

SMALL MUSHROOM
CAP
Using K, make a magic ring.
Round 1: 6sc in ring. *(6 sc)*
Round 2: 2sc in each st. *(12 sc)*
Round 3: [1sc, 2sc in next st] 6 times. *(18 sc)*
Rounds 4 and 5: 1sc in each st.
Fasten off and sew in ends.

STALK
Using F, make a magic ring.
Round 1: 6sc in ring. *(6 sc)*
Round 2: 2scBLO in each st. *(12 sc)*
Rounds 3-6: 1sc in each st.

asten off leaving long tail to sew to inside of cap,
ew in ends.

OSES

LOWER
nake 3 in L, 2 in M)
h25.

ow 1: 1dc in 5th ch from hook (counts as 1dc, ch2),
miss next ch, (1dc, ch2, 1dc) in next ch; rep from
9 times, turn. *(11 v-sts)*

ow 2: Ch1, 6dc in first 2ch sp, *1sc between next 2 dc,
dc in next 2-ch sp; rep from * to end. *(11 petals)*
asten off leaving a long tail.

EAVES
nake 8 in N, 11 in O)
h9.

ound 1: 1sc in second ch from hook, 1hdc, 1dc, 2tr,
dc, 1hdc, 3sc in last ch, working along other side
f chain, 1hdc, 1dc, 2tr, 1dc, 1hdc, 1sc, slst in beg ch.
asten off and sew in ends.

SUNSHINE
(make 2)
Using K, make a magic ring.

Round 1: 6sc in ring. *(6 sc)*
Round 2: 2sc in each st. *(12 sc)*
Round 3: [1sc, 2sc in next st] 6 times. *(18 sc)*
Round 4: [2sc, 2sc in next st] 6 times. *(24 sc)*
Round 5: [3sc, 2sc in next st] 6 times *(30 sc)*
Round 6: [4sc, 2sc in next st] 6 times *(36 sc)*
Fasten off K, join J.
With both pieces WS tog, work Round 7 through
both layers to join.
Stuff with fiber filling before closing.

Round 7: *Slst, [1sc, ch3, 1sc] in next st, rep from
* 17 times, slst in first st.
Fasten off and sew in ends.

FINISHING
Sew hat on gnome's head and beard below nose.
Sew arms and legs to body.
Roll each rose from one end and stitch in place.
Using photo as a guide, stitch gnome, sunshine,
leaves, roses, and mushrooms in place.
Tie twine across wreath to make washing line.
Peg washing to line.

techniques

This section guides you through all the crochet and finishing techniques that you will need to make the projects in this book. If you're new to crochet, practice the skills covered in this section before you start on a project. Keep the loops of your stitches loose—you can work on creating an even gauge (see page 117) across the fabric as you practice and develop your skills. Crochet has only a few basic stitches to master, and it is easy to undo if you go wrong because you only have one loop on the hook.

Holding the hook

Pick up your hook as though you are picking up a pen or pencil. Keeping the hook held loosely between your fingers and thumb, turn your hand so that the palm is facing up and the hook is balanced in your hand and resting in the space between your index finger and your thumb.

You can also hold the hook like a knife—this may be easier if you are working with a large hook or with bulky yarn. Choose the method that you find most comfortable.

Holding the yarn

1 Pick up the yarn with your little finger in the opposite hand to your hook, with your palm facing upward and with the short end in front. Turn your hand to face downward, with the yarn on top of your index finger and under the other two fingers and wrapped right around the little finger, as shown above.

2 Turn your hand to face you, ready to hold the work in your middle finger and thumb. Keeping your index finger only at a slight curve, hold the work or the slip knot using the same hand, between your middle finger and your thumb and just below the crochet hook and loop/s on the hook.

Holding the hook and yarn while crocheting

Keep your index finger, with the yarn draped over it, at a slight curve, and hold your work (or the slip knot) using the same hand, between your middle finger and your thumb and just below the crochet hook and loop/s on the hook.

As you draw the loop through the hook release the yarn on the index finger to allow the loop to stay loose on the hook. If you tense your index finger, the yarn will become too tight and pull the loop on the hook too tight for you to draw the yarn through.

Holding the hook and yarn for left-handers

Some left-handers learn to crochet like right-handers, but others learn with everything reversed—with the hook in the left hand and the yarn in the right.

Making a slip knot

The simplest way is to make a circle with the yarn, so that the loop is facing downward.

In one hand hold the circle at the top where the yarn crosses, and let the tail drop down at the back so that it falls across the center of the loop. With your free hand or the tip of a crochet hook, pull a loop through the circle.

2 Put the hook into the loop and pull gently so that it forms a loose loop on the hook.

Yarn over hook (yoh)

To create a stitch, catch the yarn from behind with the hook pointing upward. As you gently pull the yarn through the loop on the hook, turn the hook so it faces downward and slide the yarn through the loop. The loop on the hook should be kept loose enough for the hook to slide through easily.

Magic ring

This is a useful starting technique if you do not want a visible hole in the center of your round. Loop the yarn over your finger, insert the hook through the ring, yarn over hook, pull through the ring to make the first chain. Work the number of stitches required into the ring and then pull the end to tighten the center ring and close the hole.

Chain (ch)

1 Using the hook, wrap the yarn over the hook ready to pull it through the loop on the hook.

2 Pull through, creating a new loop on the hook. Continue in this way to create a chain of the required length.

Counting chains

To count chains in a foundation chain, lay the chain out on a flat surface with the right side facing you and count each "V" as one chain. Always count chains from the front of the chain (the end nearest to the hook) and do not count the loop on the hook as one chain.

6 5 4 3 2 1

Chain ring

If you are crocheting a round shape, one way of starting off is by crocheting a number of chains following the instructions in your pattern, and then joining them into a circle.

1 Using the hook, wrap the yarn over the hook ready to pull it through the loop on the hook.

2 Pull the yarn through the chain and through the loop on your hook at the same time, thereby creating a slip stitch and forming a circle. You now have a chain ring ready to work stitches into as instructed in the pattern.

Chain space (ch sp)

1 A chain space is the space that has been made under a chain in the previous round or row, and falls in between other stitches.

2 Stitches into a chain space are made directly into the hole created under the chain and not into the chain stitches themselves.

Making rows

When making straight rows you turn the work at the end of each row and make a turning chain to create the height you need for the stitch you are working with, as for making rounds.

Single crochet = 1 chain
Half double crochet = 2 chains
Double crochet = 3 chains
Treble = 4 chains

Making rounds

When working in rounds the work is not turned, so you are always working from one side. Depending on the pattern you are working, a "round" can be square. Start each round by making one or more chains to create the height you need for the stitch you are working:

Single crochet = 1 chain
Half double crochet = 2 chains
Double crochet = 3 chains
Treble = 4 chains

Work the required stitches to complete the round. At the end of the round, slip stitch into the top of the chain to close the round.

Continous spiral

If you work in a spiral you do not need a turning chain. After completing the base ring, place a stitch marker in the first stitch and then continue to croche around. When you have made a round and reached the point where the stitch marker is, work this stitch, take out the stitch marker from the previous round and put it back into the first stitch of the new round. A safety pin or piece of yarn in a contrasting color makes a good stitch marker.

Slip stitch (sl st)

A slip stitch doesn't create any height and is often used as the last stitch to create a smooth and even round or row.

1 To make a slip stitch: first put the hook through the work, yarn over hook.

2 Pull the yarn through both the work and through the loop on the hook at the same time, so you will have 1 loop on the hook.

Working into top of stitch

Unless otherwise directed, always insert the hook under both of the two loops on top of the stitch—this is the standard technique.

Working into front loop of stitch (FLO)

To work into the front loop of a stitch, pick up the front loop from underneath at the front of the work.

Working into back loop of stitch (BLO)

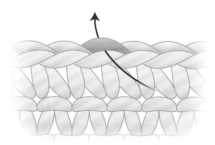

To work into the back loop of the stitch, insert the hook between the front and the back loop, picking up the back loop from the front of the work.

Back post stitch

Instead of inserting the hook under or into the 'V' of the required stitch, insert it from the back around the vertical part (the post) of the stitch from the row below.

Gauge (tension)

While specific gauge (exactly how loose or tight your crocheted fabric is) isn't essential for these projects, it's important your crocheted fabric is even and doesn't have large gaps. Before you start a project you can make a small swatch, such as 20 stitches by 20 rows in single crochet to see how the finished crocheted fabric will look with the chosen hook and yarn. If your crocheted fabric is very loose with large gaps, you'll need to use a smaller hook. If the fabric is very tight and difficult to work, use a larger hook. You can experiment by making swatches with different size hooks until you have created a crocheted fabric you're happy with. Use this hook for the project.

Single crochet (sc)

1 Insert the hook into your work, yarn over hook and pull the yarn through the work only. You will then have 2 loops on the hook.

2 Yarn over hook again and pull through the two loops on the hook. You will then have 1 loop on the hook.

Half double crochet (hdc)

1 Before inserting the hook into the work, wrap the yarn over the hook and put the hook through the work with the yarn wrapped around.

2 Yarn over hook again and pull through the first loop on the hook. You now have 3 loops on the hook.

3 Yarn over hook and pull the yarn through all 3 loops. You will be left with 1 loop on the hook.

Double crochet (dc)

1 Before inserting the hook into the work, wrap the yarn over the hook. Put the hook through the work with the yarn wrapped around, yarn over hook again and pull through the first loop on the hook. You now have 3 loops on the hook.

2 Yarn over hook again, pull the yarn through the first 2 loops on the hook. You now have 2 loops on the hook.

3 Yarn over hook, pull the yarn through 2 loops again. You will be left with 1 loop on the hook.

Treble (tr)

Yarn over hook twice, insert the hook into the stitch, yarn over hook, pull a loop through (4 loops on hook), yarn over hook, pull the yarn through 2 stitches (3 loops on hook), yarn over hook, pull a loop through the next 2 stitches (2 loops on hook), yarn over hook, pull a loop through the last 2 stitches. You will be left with 1 loop on the hook.

Increasing

Make two or three stitches into one stitch or space from the previous row. The illustration shows a double crochet increase being made.

Decreasing

You can decrease by either missing the next stitch and continuing to crochet, or by crocheting two or more stitches together. The basic technique for crocheting stitches together is the same, no matter which stitch you are using. The following example shows sc2tog.

Single crochet two stitches together (sc2tog)

1 Insert the hook into your work, yarn over hook and pull the yarn through the work (2 loops on hook). Insert the hook in next stitch, yarn over hook and pull the yarn through.

2 Yarn over hook again and pull through all 3 loops on the hook. You will then have 1 loop on the hook.

Joining yarn at the end of a row or round

You can use this technique when changing color, or when joining in a new ball of yarn as one runs out.

1 Keep the loop of the old yarn on the hook. Drop the tail and catch a loop of the strand of the new yarn with the crochet hook.

2 Draw the new yarn through the loop on the hook, keeping the old loop drawn tight and continue as instructed in the pattern.

Joining in new yarn after fastening off

1 Fasten off the old color (see below). Make a slip knot with the new color (see page 115). Insert the hook into the stitch at the beginning of the next row, then through the slip knot.

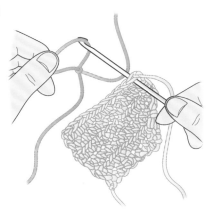

2 Draw the loop of the slip knot through to the front of the work. Carry on working using the new color, following the instructions in the pattern.

Enclosing a yarn tail

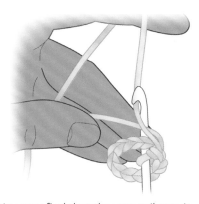

You may find that the yarn tail gets in the way as you work; you can enclose this into the stitches as you go by placing the tail at the back as you wrap the yarn. This also saves having to sew this tail end in later.

Fastening off

When you have finished crocheting, you need to fasten off the stitches to stop all your work unraveling.

Draw up the final loop of the last stitch to make it bigger. Cut the yarn, leaving a tail of approximately 4in (10cm)—unless a longer end is needed for sewing up. Pull the tail all the way through the loop and pull the loop up tightly.

Sewing in yarn ends

It is important to weave in the tail ends of the yarn so that they are secure and your crochet won't unravel. Thread a yarn needle with the tail end of yarn. On the wrong side, take the needle through the crochet one stitch down on the edge, then take it through the stitches, working in a gentle zig-zag. Work through four or five stitches then return in the opposite direction. Remove the needle, pull the crochet gently to stretch it and trim the end.

Blocking

Crochet can tend to curl, so to make flat pieces stay flat you may need to block them. Pin the piece out to the correct size and shape on an ironing board or some soft foam mats (such as the ones sold as children's play mats). Spray the crochet with water and leave it to dry completely before unpinning and removing from the board or mats.

Mattress stitch

Using mattress stitch creates an invisible seam that is perfect for sewing together different crocheted pieces or granny squares. It is worked from the right side.

1 Line up the two pieces—pin them together if it helps make them more secure. Thread a tail of yarn in the same color as the pieces you're joining into a yarn sewing needle. Pick up a loop on the other side with the yarn sewing needle at a horizontal angle (90 degree angle) to the pattern and draw the yarn through loosely.

2 Pick up a loop on the corresponding side of the other piece just inside the edge and draw through the yarn. Leave the loops loose and don't draw them through tightly.

3 Pick up the next loop approx ½in (1cm) along on the same side and draw through the yarn.

4 Pick up a loop on the corresponding side of the other piece just inside the edge and draw through the yarn. Leave the loops loose and don't draw them through tightly.

5 Repeat steps 3 and 4. When you have about 6 loops, hold the pieces firmly in place and pull the thread to draw the loose loops and bind the edging together.

6 Continue in this way, repeating steps 3, 4 and 5 until the seam is joined. This will create an invisible seam on the right side of the work.

Making a single crochet seam or slip stitch seam

With a single crochet seam you join two pieces together using a crochet hook and working a single crochet stitch through both pieces, instead of sewing them together with a tail of yarn and a yarn sewing needle. This makes a quick and strong seam and gives a slightly raised finish to the edging. For a less raised seam, follow the same basic technique, but work each stitch in slip stitch rather than single crochet.

1 Start by lining up the two pieces with wrong sides together. Insert the hook in the top 2 loops of the stitch of the first piece, then into the corresponding stitch on the second piece.

2 Complete the single crochet stitch as normal and continue on the next stitches as directed in the pattern. This gives a raised effect if the single crochet stitches are made on the right side of the work.

3 You can work with the wrong side of the work facing (with the pieces right side facing) if you don't want this effect and it still creates a good strong join.

Join-as-you-go method for granny squares

1 Work the first side of the current square including the first corner grouping (first set of 3hdc or 3dc), then instead of making ch2 for the corner space, insert the hook into the corner space of the starting square from underneath as shown.

2 1sc into the corner space of the starting square (counts as first of 2-ch for the corner space), ch1, then work the second 3hdc or 3dc grouping into the corner space of the current square as usual.

3 To continue joining the squares together, instead of ch1, work 1sc into the next side space of the starting square.

4 Work 3hdc or 3dc in the next side space of the current square. Continue replacing each ch-1 at the sides of the current square with 1sc into the next side space of the starting square, and replacing the first of the ch-2 at the corner space of the current square with 1sc into the corner space of the starting square.

5 When the current square is joined to the starting square along one side, continue around and finish the final round of the current square as normal.

6 When joining a current square to two previous squares, replace both corner ch of the current square with 1sc into each adjoining square.

Surface crochet

Surface crochet is a simple way to add extra decoration to a finished item, working slip stitches over the surface of the fabric.

1 Using a contrast yarn, make a slip knot (see page 115). Holding the yarn with the slip knot behind the work and the hook in front, insert the hook between two stitches from front to the back and catch the slip knot behind the work with the hook. Draw the slip knot back through, so there is 1 loop on the hook at the front of the work

2 Insert the hook between the next 2 stitches, yarn over hook and draw a loop through to the front. You will now have 2 loops on the hook.

3 Pull the first loop on the hook through the second loop to complete the first slip stitch on the surface of the work. Repeat steps 2 and 3 to make the next slip stitch. To join two ends with an invisible join, cut the yarn and thread onto a yarn needle. Insert the needle up through the last stitch, into the first stitch as if you were crocheting it, then into the back loop of the previous stitch. Fasten off on the wrong side.

Crab stitch

This is simply single crochet worked backward to give a twisted edge. Crab stitch spreads the edge slightly, so there's no need to crease to turn a corner. If a straight edge flutes, either miss the occasional stitch or use a smaller hook.

Do not turn the work at the end of the last row. Insert the hook in the last stitch to the right, yarn over hook, and pull through to make two loops twisted on the hook. Yarn over hook again and pull through making one loop on the hook. Repeat in the stitches along the edge or in row ends if necessary.

Popcorn

A popcorn differs from a cluster in that it is made up of complete stitches that are joined at the top. This example shows a popcorn made with four double crochet stitches worked into a foundation chain, but a popcorn can be worked into any stitch or space and can be made up of any practical number or combination of stitches. It is abbreviated as "PC."

1 Inserting the hook in the same place each time, work 4 complete double crochets.

2 Slip the hook out of the last loop and insert it into the top of the first stitch.

3 Then insert the hook into the loop of the last stitch again. Yarn over hook and pull it through as indicated.

4 This makes one complete popcorn.

Puff stitch

A puff stitch is a padded stitch worked by creating several loops on the hook before completing the stitch. The basic principle is always the same, but you can repeat steps 1 and 2 fewer times to make a smaller puff. Sometimes a chain is worked at the end to secure the puff. It is abbreviated as "PS."

1 Yarn over hook, and insert the hook into the next stitch or space.

2 Yarn over hook again and draw through, keeping the loops of yarn long.

3 Repeat steps 1 and 2 five more times, keeping the loops long each time. There will be 13 loops on the hook.

4 Yarn over hook and draw through all the loops on the hook.

5 Yarn over hook, and draw through the single loop on the hook to make a chain and secure the puff stitch.

Bobble

Bobbles are created when working on wrong-side rows and the bobble is then pushed out toward the right-side row. This is a four-double-crochet cluster bobble (4dcCL).

1 Yarn over hook and then insert the hook in the stitch, yarn over hook and pull the yarn through the work.

2 Yarn over hook and pull the yarn through the first 2 loops on the hook (2 loops on hook).

3 Repeat steps 1 and 2 three more times in the same stitch, yarn over hook and pull through all 5 loops on the hook.

4 You can also make 1 chain to complete the bobble.

Cluster

Clusters are groups of stitches, with each stitch only partly worked and then all joined at the top to create a particular pattern or shape. They are most effective when made using a longer stitch, such as double crochet. This is a two-double-crochet cluster, which is abbreviated as "2dcCL."

1 Yarn over hook, insert the hook in the stitch (or space).

2 Yarn over hook, pull the yarn through the work (3 loops on the hook).

3 Yarn over hook, pull the yarn through 2 loops on the hook (2 loops on the hook).

4 Yarn over hook, insert the hook in the same stitch (or space).

5 Yarn over hook, pull the yarn through the work (4 loops on the hook).

6 Yarn over hook, pull the yarn through 2 loops on the hook (3 loops on the hook).

7 Yarn over hook, pull the yarn through all 3 loops on the hook (1 loop on the hook).

Loop stitch

1 With the yarn over the left index finger, insert the hook into the next stitch and draw two strands through the stitch (take the first strand from under the index finger and at the same time take the second strand from over the index finger).

2 Pull the yarn to tighten the loop, forming a 1½-in (4-cm) loop on the index finger. Remove your finger from the loop, put the loop to the back of the work, yarn over hook and pull through 3 loops on the hook (1 loop stitch made on right side of work).

French knots

Bring the yarn needle up to the surface at the position of the knot. Holding the yarn taut, wrap it two or three times around the tip of the needle. Continue holding the yarn taut as you pass the needle back down through the fabric close to the entry point. The yarn will pull through the wraps and they will form a knot that sits on the surface of the crocheted fabric.

Crochet stitch conversion chart

Crochet stitches are worked in the same way in both the USA and the UK, but the stitch names are not the same and identical names are used for different stitches. Below is a list of the US terms used in this book, and the equivalent UK terms.

US TERM	UK TERM
single crochet (sc)	double crochet (dc)
half double crochet (hdc)	half treble (htr)
double crochet (dc)	treble (tr)
treble (tr)	double treble (dtr)
gauge	tension
yarn over hook (yoh)	yarn round hook (yrh)

Abbreviations

BLO	back loop only
BP	back post
ch	chain
ch sp	chain space
CLr	cluster
cont	continu(e)ing
dc	double crochet
FLO	front loop only
hdc	half double crochet
inc	increase
opp	opposite
PC	popcorn
prev	previous
PS	puff stitch
rep	repeat
RS	right side
sc	single crochet
sc2tog	work 2 single crochet stitches together (decrease 1 st)
slst	slip stitch
st(s)	stitch(es)
tog	together
tr	treble
WS	wrong side
yoh	yarn over hook

Suppliers

We cannot cover all stockists here, so please explore the local yarn stores and online retailers in your own country. If you wish to substitute a different yarn for the one recommended in the pattern, try the Yarnsub website for suggestions: www.yarnsub.com.

USA

LoveCrafts
Online sales
www.lovecrafts.com

Knitting Fever Inc.
www.knittingfever.com

WEBS
www.yarn.com

Jo-Ann Fabric and Craft Stores
Yarns and craft supplies
www.joann.com

Michaels
Craft supplies
www.michaels.com

UK

LoveCrafts
Online sales
www.lovecrafts.com

Wool
Yarn, hooks
Store in Bath
+44 (0)1225 469144
www.woolbath.co.uk

Wool Warehouse
Online sales
www.woolwarehouse.co.uk

Laughing Hens
Online sales
Tel: +44 (0) 1829 740903
www.laughinghens.com

John Lewis
Yarns and craft supplies
Telephone numbers of stores
on website
www.johnlewis.com

Hobbycraft
Yarns, twig wreath bases
www.hobbycraft.co.uk

Australia

Black Sheep Wool 'n' Wares
Retail store and online
Tel: +61 (0)2 6779 1196
www.blacksheepwool.com.au

Sun Spun
Retail store (Canterbury, Victoria)
and online
Tel: +61 (0)3 9830 1609
www.sunspun.com.au

Acknowledgments

Firstly, I am so very grateful for the continued support and patience from everyone involved at CICO Books. Thank you for believing in me and wanting to share my love of crochet and bright quirky designs in book form. You have made a dream of mine come true!

A huge thank you to Hobbycraft and Rico Design for all the beautiful yarn and material support needed to create my designs. It has been a pleasure as always using your gorgeous products.

I am endlessly grateful for the support of my four daughters who fill my life with pure happiness. They always want to be involved with every new project. I am so proud of them, and so very happy that they are interested in something that means so much to me.

I'd like to thank my partner, Chris, who is always more than happy to listen to my weird and crazy ideas and has supported me every step of my journey this past year. You never tire of showing interest in what I do and I am so thankful of the little pushes that you give me to achieve more of what I love.

Last but certainly not least; I am so thankful of all my yarn loving followers on my social media pages, who have supported me from day one. I am honored by every like, message, and share, every pattern and book sale. I would not be where I am now without your support.

Index